In Loving Hands

In
Loving
Hands

Kris Mackay

BOOKCRAFT / Salt Lake City, Utah

Library of Congress Catalog Card Number: 85-72076
ISBN 0-88494-566-9

First Printing, 1985

Printed in the United States of America

To Bud Gardner,
who takes a classroom
full of hopeful beginners
and convinces us all
we are writers.

Contents

1

In Loving Hands

Len Foote's neck was broken, so it was important that he lie perfectly still.

He had just been moved—slowly and carefully, bed and all—from Intensive Care, where dedicated nurses had hovered over him constantly. Now he was lying in a private room in the hospital's orthopedic section, where the nurses were still dedicated but procedures were different. Now nobody sat at his bedside every hour of the day and night. It was the first time since the accident that he'd been left alone for a second, and he was terrified to relax and go to sleep.

It was imperative that he remain completely motionless. He could manage that while he was awake. But what if some overwrought muscle twitched or jerked involuntarily in his sleep?

His third cervical vertebra was crushed and fragmented, and dozens of tiny, sharp pieces were floating perilously close to his spinal cord. Surgery was too dangerous to consider. The order given was for him to remain perfectly still, allowing those fragments the months of quiet they needed in order to knit together again.

The doctor's voice had been soft, but his parting words were chilling: "Remember—if you move, you could be paralyzed for life!"

Len knew what that entailed. He thought of a favorite cousin who was paralyzed in a bodysurfing accident when only eighteen. His cousin handled it well and had, in fact, been an inspiration to everyone who knew him. Nevertheless the prospect of spending the rest of his life in a wheelchair was a prospect Len viewed with total and absolute horror.

Accidents happen so quickly. Len had pulled away from the high council meeting at the stake center near Rancho Cordova, California, about 9:20 P.M. He drove his light, imported pickup down Highway 50, expecting to reach home in less than twenty minutes.

He eased to a stop behind another car at the intersection where city and county lines met. Perhaps that joining of authority accounts for road markings not being as clear as they might be. Motorists unfamiliar with that spot can be momentarily confused.

Len traveled that highway often. Idling the motor, waiting for the red signal to switch to green, he noticed car lights in his rearview mirror. He remembers they were coming up fast. That's all he does remember until he came to, sprawled across the steering wheel, feeling the trickle of blood oozing down his back. He couldn't move.

A gruff male voice was swearing crudely in his ear, accusing him of somehow causing the pileup. All Len could manage was the most fragile of whispers: "I'm hurt!"

His truck was totaled. Rammed violently from behind, it shoved forward to slam into the car ahead and jackknifed between the two; the mortally wounded pickup and its helpless passenger bore the brunt of the impact. Len's head shot backwards and crashed through the rear window, then ricocheted ahead to also smash through the windshield. His spine was crushed against the metal surrounding the rear window.

But from the beginning, someone had been there to protect him against damaging movement. At first it was an off-duty nurse who leaped from her own car into the left lane in her haste to reach his side. As he came to, he was aware of a woman's cool hands holding his head in place where it lay, and he heard her voice say sharply, "Don't touch him! Don't anybody touch him!"

Firemen, highway patrol officers, and the general curious public milled around trying their best to help, but the nurse was equally firm with all of them. When an ambulance came, she insisted on supervising his removal.

Somebody he knew well arrived at the scene, although Len didn't recognize him at the time. Joe Hodgson, second counselor in the Sacramento Cordova Stake presidency and home teacher to the Foote family, had been the last one to leave the council meeting. He drove away from the parking lot two to three minutes behind the others, heading east on Highway 50 in the direction Len had already taken.

President Hodgson was alarmed when he saw the accident. He jumped from his car and ran to peer inside the mangled pickup. Then he breathed a sigh of personal relief and muttered to himself, "At least it's not one of our people." That lack of recognition of either the truck or his good and longtime friend indicates the shape both were in when he saw them.

President Hodgson had no idea as he turned back to his car that before midnight he would stand in the X-ray room of a local hospital, hastily administering an emergency priesthood blessing to that same battered but unrecognizable friend.

The injured man in the X-ray room had willed himself not to lose consciousness. It was important that he be aware of what took place.

Alone now for the first time in his private room, now when he wanted—needed—to sleep and couldn't, he found it almost amusing to think back to how he'd forced himself to stay awake during the blessing. He simply couldn't allow himself to black out. He had to listen to the words of the prayer.

He'd been on the giving side of administration often enough to have a hearty respect for the inspiration received when men with proper authority lay their hands on heads of the sick or injured. He needed to hear if Joe Hodgson and Dana Dyer, the latter from the high council, could promise that he would recover.

Recovery, yes—but had they promised he wouldn't be *paralyzed*? Looking back and trying to sort it all out in his weary mind, he didn't recall *that* word being mentioned.

He was definitely drowsy. He thought about his faithful wife, Lettie, who arrived at his side every morning at eight and didn't leave again until nine at night when she went home to the children. He concentrated on trying to go to sleep because rest was so important in his condition. Nervous tension was the last thing he should have. The problem was that every time he began to drift off, fear of moving shocked him as wide awake as if he'd suddenly been doused with a bucket of cold water.

Precautions had been taken against the possibility of movement. His bed was a Stryker frame consisting of two pieces of metal held together by strips of canvas. It was seldom used, and they'd had to dig it out of storage. It was a stretcher-like arrangement barely wider than he was. He'd seen one once in a movie.

Periodically during the day an identical frame was bolted

down snugly over the top of his body so that medical technicians could change his position with a cautious flip-flop. Leather straps across the chin and forehead held his head securely in place as he was turned. He ate his meals in that strange upside-down position.

Tension to stretch his neck was supplied by a rounded metal yoke over the top of his head that ended in screws with razor-sharp cutting edges which were screwed into his skull bone directly over each ear. A twelve-pound weight hung by rope from the middle of the yoke. Doctors warned against a natural tendency to slide upwards in bed in response to that weight. Effect of the tension would be nullified if his neck bones went slack.

So Len had a lot to worry him.

In Intensive Care his head and neck had been sandbagged, and a strap around his hips reminded him—even in sleep—to stay exactly where he was. Most of those safeguards (other than the sandbags) were still in place in this new room, except that now, after Lettie left, the human element was missing. The nurse's station was located outside his door and a nurse could reach his side in seconds if he called. Still, there was nobody *in* the room to monitor him constantly if he drifted off, someone who cared enough to make certain he didn't inadvertently move.

Len shut his eyes and tried his best to relax.

Suddenly, he felt the wonderfully comforting feeling of hands cradling the back and sides of his head. He hadn't heard anyone come in. Could it be that his muscles merely remembered earlier support of the sandbags?

He opened his eyes. His stepfather stood at the foot of the bed. It seemed perfectly natural, although they hadn't seen each other since Len was called to Arizona ten years earlier to help put affairs in order before his stepfather died of cancer. He remembered the sadness of that time as if it were yesterday.

But the personage in the room wasn't tired or old or sad, as he had been the day they hugged and said their last farewell. This was a man in his prime—tall, vigorous, and very handsome—and he radiated with light.

He didn't seem to be aware that Len could see him. All his attention was focused on the space behind Len's head, on whoever it was that so lovingly held Len, and his face bore a look of tender concern.

Len couldn't turn his head to search behind him with his mortal eyes, of course, but he didn't need to. He knew as surely as if he *had* turned that his father was standing there—his natural father who had died when Len was six, a man he had worshipped as a boy. When his mother remarried, he and his new father shared the same kind of attachment. What could be more logical than the two men who loved him most joining forces and coming at a time when their son's whole future hung on what happened to him now?

Len was no longer frightened. He slipped into deep, peaceful slumber that he was able to duplicate at will for the rest of his eight-week hospital stay.

His stepfather didn't appear to him again. There was no need. During the period of immobility necessary for a full and total recovery, Len never once doubted that his safety—and his future—lay in loving hands.

2

The Death of a Friend

I've had an emotional hangup concerning death, and the passing of our baby at two days old made it worse, I'm afraid. The tenacity of that hangup bothered me.

The plan of salvation is very real to me, and I believe it with all my heart. So when friends attempted to console me with all the tried and true phrases—such as "He was too pure to have to be tested in this life" and "You know you'll have a chance to raise him in the next"—why couldn't I be comforted?

Alta Malan and I sat visiting in her living room. We'd finished an interview on another subject, and I now began to gather up my papers and tape recorder and prepared to leave.

But I make it a practice never to stand up and actually move to the door immediately after an interview is completed. I linger, and we chat. Often some of the most intense conversations or most enlightening facts emerge after the person interviewed thinks our purpose is accomplished. Though I try to interview on an informal basis, it could be that some slight, residual feeling of being on display keeps the atmosphere from being totally relaxed. After my notebook is closed and my pen placed securely back into my purse, we often find ourselves speaking on a different level altogether.

That's how it was on that particular day. I don't recall exactly how the subject of death came up, or which of us initiated it. I only know that before I realized what was happening, Alta—a woman I had known for years and admired tremendously—was earnestly describing to me what took place *when she died.*

Her experience also involved a baby (her second), except that in her case it wasn't the baby who was ill, it was she.

Six weeks after delivery she developed a sudden, life-threatening infection and was rushed by ambulance back to the hospital she'd recently left. There, all the medical technology available in a modern healing establishment was called into play in a concentrated effort to save her.

At one point she was alone with a nurse. Suddenly the nurse stiffened, gasped, and then dashed from the room. She returned with the doctor, who worked with great speed checking and rechecking the patient. Then Alta clearly heard him pronounce her dead.

Hearing him say she was gone was a curious sensation to Alta, of course. How was it she could see and hear him if she was dead? Even stranger (and she hesitated on this part, looking at me with a timid, apologetic smile), she wasn't lying unconscious on the bed inside of the lifeless body, but seemed to be watching from somewhere up above where she could easily observe.

I didn't realize the full significance of her statement at the time. Five months earlier, I had listened spellbound during an all-day seminar on death and dying conducted by Dr. Elisabeth Kubler-Ross, the world's foremost secular authority on the subject. Interviews with hundreds of patients who had returned to life after "near-death" experiences formed the basis of her research. Everything she described about the state of the spirit after death fit hand in glove into what I believed—intellectually—to be fact.

But mostly she concentrated on her work with dying patients and the need to comfort their families. She didn't delve as deeply as I'd hoped she would into research with those "near-death" situations. She did tell us about a Dr. William Moody, and that his book *Life After Life*—actual, documented case histories of individuals who had experienced death and returned to tell their stories—would be available in stores in approximately six months. Dr. Moody's publishers wanted prepublication verification of detail, and the book was sent to Dr. Kubler-Ross to edit. It didn't need editing. We at the seminar were interested to hear her say that Dr. Moody's research resembled hers exactly; she could have written every word of his manuscript.

But the book wasn't out yet, and hardly any information it contained had by then been made public. Alta had no way of knowing that her description to me that day constituted a classic example of what secular research insists occurs during the first few minutes after a spirit separates from its body.

From her position "somewhere up above," she watched them draw the sheet over the face of her dead body and heard the doctor discuss making out the death certificate.

As he left the room, her horizons expanded. For the first time she noticed she was next to some type of curtain or veil of overwhelming whiteness. Instinctively she recognized the veil as a boundary. All she needed to do was reach out her hand, draw the fabric aside, and step through. And oh, how she *wanted* to be on the other side!

Again Alta hesitated in her description. Words were simply

not available in her human vocabulary to help me understand the brightness of the curtain. Nor the blinding light pouring through it that should have hurt her eyes, but didn't. Nor the glorious, soul-nourishing sound of music issuing forth from behind it.

I was especially curious at her mention of music. Being a ward choir director, I questioned her about that. Was the music vocal, and if so could she understand or remember the words?

Alta remembered it perfectly. I was impressed with the clarity of her remembrance. Two months later Dr. Moody's book was in print, and I read his published belief that events experienced in the spirit are never forgotten. Details are as clear twenty, forty, or sixty years later as they were the minute after they took place.

That's how it was with Alta. The music she described didn't involve singing. But once again—though her mind had total recall—she stumbled over lack of appropriate words. The closest she could come to answering my question to her own satisfaction was to liken what she heard to the finest symphonies the world has ever created—except that she couldn't identify a few of the instruments, and the sound they produced was infinitely more exquisite than any master symphony she'd ever enjoyed.

The light, the music, and most of all an encompassing *love* of a quality she'd never before experienced, emanated through the curtain. She eagerly started forward. Listening intently, I sensed her *longing* even as she spoke, years later, with her three boys grown and with homes and families of their own. We sat quietly together in her living room, but the expression in her eyes told me she was far away in another time and place.

With one hand clutching the veil, she had stopped. She thought of her babies. They needed her. Realization that it wasn't her time, that she was needed on earth and must return, took root and began to grow stronger. Even so, every instinct of her being propelled her to move the curtain aside and step through.

Instead she drifted backwards. Imperceptibly. It was as if a silken thread attached to her shoulders drew her back inch by inch toward the body she had discarded and which still lay lifeless on the hospital bed.

Four years after our conversation Alta *did* pass away, finally and irrevocably this time. I went to the funeral, but try as I might, I couldn't generate a feeling of sadness.

The chapel was filled to overflowing and the service was beautiful, I'm sure, although to this day I can't repeat the words of the speakers. Their voices were drowned out for me by my memory of Alta's voice saying, "It was years before I could look at anything white without having it appear dingy to my eyes."

I'd pull my attention back to the eulogy, only to have the speaker's words overpowered again by, "It was years before I could listen to my beautiful stereo without the music sounding tinny, like an assault to my ears."

No, I couldn't mourn for Alta. I would miss her. She was an exceptional woman and a dear and trusted friend, but she knew from personal experience where she was going, and it was where she had wanted—no, *yearned*—to be.

I left the chapel that morning with a modified and much more comfortable concept of death.

3

Three Inches from Life

As he pulled on his tight wet suit that early morning of July 14, 1982, twenty-four-year-old Michael Astle had no premonition of danger. He tugged at the thick, clinging rubber, worked it over his hips and up onto his shoulders, and grumbled under his breath, "Darned nuisance! If the water weren't so cold, I wouldn't bother with this uncomfortable thing."

But even as he objected, he knew the suit was a necessary part of his equipment. Nobody could stay under very long without protection against the bone-chilling river.

The author's story of this remarkable rescue was first published in the *Reader's Digest,* November 1985.

Mike looked forward to these excursions. So did his twenty-six-year-old cousin and best buddy David Burgess. They were serious "weekend" prospectors dredging for gold—at the top of California's mountains, in the heart of the 1800s gold rush country, where they were virtually alone with the hills and the sweet scent of the pines. That's the way they liked it. These two young men grew up hunting, fishing, and camping together, and they welcomed the loneliness of those hills.

Attaching weights to his waist to offset the buoyancy of the suit, Mike's mind drifted back to how he and Dave got started. They'd eased gradually into their exciting hobby of searching for gold. First they panned for it, always on the north fork of the American River ten miles above the little town of Auburn, then five miles farther up a lonely, winding, dirt road.

They always set up camp seventy yards upstream from old Shirttail-Foresthill Bridge. It was scenic country. The bridge wasn't situated directly over the water. It towered overhead, seventy-five feet higher than the river, spanning the distance between peaks. In case of a flood, the bridge wouldn't be washed away.

They worked that remote spot consistently because they'd learned from experience that bits of gold do lie buried in its cracks and crevices. After every trip they carried minute amounts of it home.

Mike chuckled. Gold mining is addictive, and he suspected both he and Dave were thoroughly hooked. A few flecks of the precious metal sparkling from their pans and they had been goners.

But before long, panning no longer satisfied the young prospectors' healthy appetites for adventure. They bought second-hand parts and little by little pieced together a fullsized dredging machine with an eight horsepower engine and pump, sluice boxes, baffle box, and six-foot flotation pontoons. He was proud of their equipment. Their four-inch hose extended twenty feet into the water and was capable of sucking up eighty to ninety gallons per minute, which translates into a powerful operation that could empty a swimming pool in minutes.

Mike called companionably to Dave, who was heading toward the river, "Hey, pal—pretty good job we did, putting all this stuff together!"

Dave wasn't wearing a wet suit that day. He wouldn't be in the water long enough to need one. Today Mike would assume the underwater position, completely submerged, guiding their powerful suction hose over sand and gravel at the bottom of the six-foot hole they'd sucked out the afternoon before. Dave's job was to wade in and out, to wrestle a rock up onto the bank or help Mike move one too big to handle on his own.

Mike moved slowly and deliberately down the bank and into the water, picking his way carefully between boulders. With water leveling out chest-high, he reached for their dredger, already bobbing on the surface. He started the engine and double-checked the sluice boxes, where tons of dirt and hopefully bits of gold blowing through the hose would be separated. Gold is heavy—six to seven times as heavy as anything else liable to shoot up through the hose, and it would sink to containers at the bottom of the boxes. Mike grinned in satisfaction. Everything seemed to be in perfect working order.

Then instinctively, almost without conscious thought, he checked again on Dave's whereabouts. "Are you okay, buddy?" he called against the roar of the dredger. "Think you can make it without a wet suit?"

Dave smiled and waved. "Sure, I'm fine. Don't worry about me!"

Mike *did* worry about Dave, and he knew Dave felt the same way about him. They were more than just cousins whose mothers happened to be sisters. They had a lot in common, including having donated two years of their lives to their church as Mormon missionaries—Mike in Ohio and Dave in Colorado.

Maybe worry was too strong a word. Concern. That was it. Concern for the other guy's welfare. Dredging for gold invariably contains *some* element of danger. Whenever masses of earth are shifted about after lying undisturbed for eons of time, the reaction of surrounding earth is difficult to predict. They both knew that.

But their years of campouts in the wilderness had formed a bond of trust and reliance on each other's reactions in times of stress that was unusually strong, even between brothers.

They took up their assigned stations and worked steadily for the next thirty minutes.

Dave was on shore when he first heard the rumble. For that first paralyzing instant he couldn't force his body to move.

Mike was completely submerged. Sounds are magnified under water. Mike heard it coming in a sudden crashing, deafening roar. At first he was puzzled. *What's that noise— thunder?* Then with a sick feeling of impending doom, he recognized what the sound meant. *That's got to be a boulder—a big one! It must weigh thousands of pounds!*

Moving rapidly in a wet suit isn't easy. Now, with the need to move fast, Mike felt as awkward as a tightly wrapped mummy. Constriction of his muscles and friction of the water against the rubber didn't allow for that kind of speed.

Down under, it wasn't his own safety he was worried about. His first horrified concern was for his cousin. *I've got to get up there,* he frantically told himself. *That rock's going to hit Dave!*

Mike kicked, crawled, and clawed his way to the top. His head broke the surface just in time to see his cousin spin around to face the oncoming monster and to watch it strike him directly with a crushing blow to the chest. Dave was flipped over backwards into the river on impact. Screaming,

"No! *No!*", his cries were stifled by water when he sank beneath the boulder's terrible weight.

He and the rock came to rest with Dave's feet at the bottom of the six-foot cone-shaped excavation, his back wedged into a rough gouge on its side in a stretched-out sitting position— with the massive boulder lying solidly on top. The crushing weight on his lap securely and effectively pinned down both of his legs.

Frigid water closed over his head, separating him, ironically, by only three to four inches from the oxygen he needed already. Panic set in. He held his breath and tried desperately to squirm out from under. But it was no use. *Mike, help me!* he silently begged. *I can't get out. Do something— quick!*

The force of the splash hurtled Mike back against the opposite bank. For a second he was almost dazed. Then came the all-consuming—"Oh, God! Help me to save Dave!"

Downstream, digging with a small hand tool in the dirt under old Shirttail-Foresthill Bridge, Steve Hagar lifted his head. He listened intently, then called to fellow miner Bob Ellis. "Did you hear something? Was that a falling boulder?" Bob answered absentmindedly. "I didn't hear anything, but what if it was? Boulders are always sliding in this part of the woods."

Steve remained motionless, listening for another five seconds. Then he shrugged. "Probably my imagination. How could we hear *anything* with that upstream dredger making such a racket?"

He lowered his head and went back to his crevicing.

Mike knew he had to act with frantic haste and instinct. There wasn't time to formulate a plan. Screaming, "Help! Somebody—help us!" he slid back into the hole. He remembered seeing two men downstream earlier that morning. *Are they still there? Did they hear me?*

But even as he shouted, louder than he'd ever called out before in his life—screaming until the sound tore at his throat—he knew they wouldn't hear him. That part of the American River slashes through a canyon where steep, almost-vertical cliffs soar up abruptly on either side. The ear-shattering drone of the dredger reverberated against the echoing hills and would make hearing him impossible. He spoke to himself sternly: "Well, Mike—it's all up to you."

Mike plunged to the bottom and stood by Dave's side. Digging his heels deep into the riverbed and with both arms outstretched, he leaned with all his weight against the weight of Dave's captor, then turned to face him, the look in his eyes crying in frustration, *It's not working! Dave, the rock won't budge!*

They didn't need words to communicate. The expression of terror on Dave's face told Mike that he grasped what Mike was struggling not to admit, even to himself—that freeing Dave by themselves was hopeless. Mike is solidly built, but both men understood that their combined all-out efforts were no match for the unyielding rock.

Mike wore underwater Hooka gear for breathing—an air hose attached to the dredger and powered by a compressor. He tore the mouthpiece from his own lips, where it had functioned all along without a hitch, and inserted it quickly into David's. *Breathe into this, Dave. This will keep you alive until I figure some way out of this mess!*

Dave grabbed onto the hose and tried to suck in. No air was available! For some unidentified reason, the regulator suddenly—at that precise moment—ceased to function.

With a fresh burst of energy born of desperation, Dave renewed his efforts to pull free. With his mind beginning to blur, he took stock of his situation. No longer could he stop his burning lungs from taking in water. Against all his efforts, he felt it clogging his nose and gurgling as it slid down his throat.

Then something closed inside his throat and instead of drowning, he was suffocating—suffocating for lack of air that hung in abundance barely over the top of his head. *It's so close,* he agonized. *I can look up and see sunlight sparkling against the surface. I raise my hands and feel the air on my fingers. There's got to be some way I can stretch to reach it!* But there was no way out.

With arms flailing wildly, he slipped into a new depth of despair. He sensed his movements were becoming uncoordinated. At that moment, with a new emotion verging almost on surprise, he faced the impossible thought head-on: *I'm really going to die!*

And yet David couldn't give up. He felt an enormous urgency to survive. Somehow he had to live! His thoughts were blurred and unconnected, but he clung to familiar images. *Laurie.* He could picture her face floating before him. *Laurie— so pretty. Prettiest girl I ever saw.* And then, weaker still, *Baby's room—not finished yet. Haven't finished painting the crib.*

His wife, Laurie, was five months pregnant with their first child. The shock of that impression jolted him back to awareness. *Oh, Lord—don't let me die now, here in this deserted hole I helped to create. I'll never get to see my baby's face!* He pulled harder and twisted. Darkness was creeping over him, but as long as he could hold on to consciousness, he'd fight to rejoin his wife and child.

Then, with a groggy, *Well, I guess this is it . . . ,* he was no longer conscious.

Mike's back was turned. He pried at the stone with a small crowbar used earlier that morning. *How much longer can Dave possibly hold on?* Turning his head to wildly search his cousin's face, he saw that it was already too late. His worst fears had just been realized.

The drowning man's skin shone with a ghostly bluish-white pallor and his lips had turned purple. But his eyes! They were wide open, but dilated, fixed in an unseeing, glassy stare, and all of his frantic thrashing movements had stopped.

He's dead! Mike told himself in a frenzy of paralyzing grief. *No! I can't accept that! What can I say to Laurie? There's got to be something more I can try!*

He kicked his way back to the surface and pulled himself over to the dredger. As he flipped the switch to stifle the raucous roar of the engine he was shrieking: "Help! Help! Isn't anybody out there? H-e-e-l-l-l-p!"

Steve Hagar and Bob Ellis keep a protective eye on each other. Miners as a group are generally like that—friendly and helpful. Regulars have a pretty fair idea where other regulars are on any given day, and they keep a neighborly watch over the other fellow's gear—always keeping one ear open for sounds of unexpected trouble. Their philosophy is, "Who knows when *we* might need somebody fast?"

Steve and Bob are totally committed to this lonely miner's life. They stay in the mountains year-round, living out of their trucks and supporting themselves on what they wrest from the ground. They don't stay together permanently, but occasionally their paths cross at the historic old suspension bridge near Shirttail Creek, where flat spots on the road lend themselves to overnight parking. Either there or at the Pioneer Mining Supplies store in downtown Auburn. Arnie Arnold, the proprietor, is a mining enthusiast himself and doesn't object to taking and delivering messages. He and his store form a major link between prospectors—and between prospectors and civilization. This remote area would be considerably harder to cope with without Arnie.

Steve's head jerked up for the second time. The dredger's noisy engine had stopped, and in sudden, eerie silence, he heard Mike's hysterical cries.

"That *was* a boulder I heard!" Steve yelled. "Let's go!" And dropping everything, he ran. Bob was right behind him.

Reaching the excavation in seconds, they gasped involuntarily and felt the blood almost freeze in their veins. There, just below the surface, his arms floating outward, his eyes staring and ghostly, was the body of a man. Seeing a dead man pinned under a rock would be bad enough in any case. But those glazed eyes staring up at them with no hint of life were indefinitely more terrifying when viewed through the distortions of running water.

Steve shuddered, almost out of control. "That guy will never make it!" Bob could barely force the words past his lips: "He's dead already!"

Nevertheless, their feet hit the water running, and as the river rose up to swallow them in one gulp, Steve uttered a quick, silent prayer for this stranger.

Within seconds all three—Mike, Bob and Steve—were pushing at the rock. Still it wouldn't move.

Bob and Joyce Dorr don't stay in the mountains during the winter. They live in the small nearby town of Georgetown, but it's customary for Bob to have a month, two months, or all summer off between jobs as a refrigeration engineer. When they do have free time, they head for the hills.

Somewhat older than miners who make prospecting their fulltime career, the Dorrs are particularly compassionate and protective of their friends. In the cold of winter, they drive over to check on each individual's welfare, and to make sure before Christmas and Easter that everybody has someplace to eat holiday dinner.

Parked in their camper on the far side of the bridge, Bob and Joyce were finishing the last bites of a leisurely breakfast. Suddenly chilling cries for help reached them from somewhere across the canyon. They couldn't see the person who called; they were camped too far away and not in a straight line of vision. They had no idea if the caller was someone they knew. But they recognized a tone of utter hysteria, and it galvanized them to action as surely as if they'd been hit with a bolt of raw electric current.

Bob's fork dropped onto his plate with a clatter and he raced outside. His feet were bare—he makes it a practice never to slip shoes on until he's ready to step out of the door—but he didn't notice the jagged pebbles tearing at his skin.

He hurtled across the bridge and down the steep, rocky trail with Joyce running, too, and screaming at the top of her lungs. "Help! Help! Can anybody hear me? Come on! We need help!" She couldn't stop herself. Besides, it was a long shot— but possible—that someone else might be camped within the sound of her voice. Something warned her that before the next few minutes were over, they would welcome all the help they could get.

Bob splashed down into the river, but Joyce stepped off to the side. She was trembling from exertion and shock. Convinced she didn't possess the muscle power to effectively push against the rock, she sank weakly to the ground. The best thing she could do for all concerned was to stay out of their way. And to pray.

She didn't bow her head because she couldn't tear her eyes from the grisly scene. *Our Father who art in heaven . . .*

Joe Sule was annoyed. Three days earlier he and two friends had driven up from southern California, parked their van on the Colfax side of the bridge near Shirttail Creek, and set up their camp a considerable distance downriver. They were prepared to go to work. Now, suddenly, their dredger's engine wouldn't work.

"Sorry, guys," he decided reluctantly. "Before we can do any more dredging we'll have to take our engine into town to get it repaired. Hate to waste our valuable vacation, but what choice do we have?" They'd already tinkered with the motor themselves, with no success.

These three miners formed one of the most unlikely combinations of nationalities ever brought together in that section of the wilds.

Joe came to the United States from Hungary in 1975; he completed his escape to freedom by swimming across the Mura River between Yugoslavia and Austria in the middle of January. He loved his new homeland. By early 1982, he was a naturalized American citizen. He'd searched for gold up and down the American River for the past two summers. He knew that area well.

In 1980 he'd had more than his share of beginner's luck. Reaching down into the river at a particularly isolated spot, he'd scooped up a handful of finely crafted twenty-dollar gold pieces left there, apparently, from the days of the gold rush.

He was ecstatic! "There's no trick to this business of finding gold," he'd assured himself and his wife.

So in 1981, he pulled out all stops and rented a helicopter to fly in tons of equipment and dozens of helpers. The problem was that during that year's expedition he wasn't as fortunate. That time, he went home with next to nothing.

This summer he was more realistic. Preparations had been kept simple, and he'd invited only two of his friends.

Andras Szavoszt, a fellow Hungarian who worked alongside Joe in Los Angeles as a mechanic, was new to the country and had accrued only one short week of vacation. It was going fast.

Professor Krzysztof (Krys) Kleszcz was *really* a long way from home. He teaches on the faculty of the University of Krakow, Poland. Krys was in America for the first time, briefly visiting his sister in Los Angeles. Joe's wife is Polish. Krys and Joe met through the Los Angeles Polish community.

Krys doesn't speak English. Joe knew at first sight that the tall and athletic Krys must be deeply involved in sports, and he was right. Swimming and skiing are subjects Krys teaches at the university, and as a coach his background includes an extensive study of pre-med.

Joe, Andras, and Krys hiked up the winding trail and deposited the ailing engine in the back of their van, parked across the road from the Dorrs' camper. Should they crowd themselves into the van to change clothes for their trip to town, or could they risk standing out in the open? Joe glanced over at the camper. It was quiet. Obviously, nobody was home. He stripped down to his tennis shoes and undershorts.

While he was poised with one hand reaching for his shirt, Joe's ears picked up a strange sound that shouldn't have been there. He couldn't distinguish what it was. "Is that yelling, faint and far off in the distance?" he questioned his friends. They hadn't heard anything, and he wasn't sure.

For that one split second, he centered his whole concentration on listening. Maybe it was more of a feeling than an actual noise. Joe has been in the woods often enough to recognize instinctively when something upsets the delicate balance of nature.

Without a word to the others, he sped—in his underwear— across the bridge with all the speed his legs could muster. At the other end, he was able to see where the sound originated. Water was splashing upriver, and heads bobbed about unnaturally. The area radiated with tension. It was clearly the scene of a disaster.

He called to his friends hoarsely, "Come with me!" and beckoned them on before racing down the mountain. Krys and Andras leaped away from the van and followed him swiftly in his race.

Suddenly—unbelievably, considering the remoteness of their surroundings—Mike heard the jolts as three additional sets of feet pounded along the path. He felt their splash as two of the men jumped in to offer their assistance.

Andras was particularly sickened by the sight. Physically ill, he felt his stomach retch and he gasped, "I've seen dead men before, but never anything like this."

But one man didn't lend his weight in the push against the boulder. Krys hesitated at the river's edge and studied the man trapped under the water. He thought: *I can help him—I know I can! All that specific training—and here in America I'll have a chance to put it to use.*

He jumped into the water and kneeled down authoritatively on the slope by David's side. Since 1973 he'd belonged to an organization called Volunteer Life-savers' Association. Every member of the group is required to undergo formal training in an unusual method of first aid. Quickly, he reviewed the techniques of what he planned to attempt.

Then he commenced to administer *underwater* mouth-to-mouth resuscitation. He pinched the victim's nostrils shut while transferring air from his own lungs into David's apparently lifeless body. He blew with considerable force, more than would be necessary for regular resuscitation.

On hands and knees and leaning—in the water—over the unconscious head, it was a simple matter to replenish his own supply of oxygen. He slipped one hand between David's mouth and his, tipped his own head back far enough to clear the surface, and took in a great gulp of air before bending to continue.

He didn't count 1001 . . . 1002 . . . as is normal in resuscitation. Stopping between breaths to lift his head to the surface consumed at least that much time.

He knew that the lungs of drowning victims are frequently not filled with water, as one would suppose. In cases of sudden immersion in extremely cold water, especially when accompanied by mortal fright or pain, the larynx often closes and seals passage to the lungs. He blew hard enough to force his breath past that barrier.

The procedure was so simple that frenzied onlookers were

amazed they hadn't thought of it themselves. But it *was* tiring. Krys began to hyperventilate. After three to four minutes he knew he had to have help.

"Joe, the water is so cold I can't get my breath. Can you spell me off?" (All of his conversations were conducted, of course, in his native tongue.)

Joe's feet moved heavily as he waded over to take Krys's place. He was tired, too. The hectic pace of their run down the trail plus the icy quality of the water were taking their toll. But he responded without hesitation: "Sure I can. Tell me exactly what to do."

"Blow in his mouth—that's all. Nothing fancy. Just keep that air going into his lungs."

Joe felt for Dave's pulse and was gratified to feel it flutter weakly beneath his fingertips. Sucking in a deep, preliminary breath, he sighed, "At least he's still alive. Couldn't prove it from the way he looks."

Joe lowered his mouth to Dave's and drew back quickly. Coarse hair of the man's mustache and the stubble of an unshaven chin prickled his skin uncomfortably. Immediately he was ashamed at his reaction. Lowering his head again, he asked himself, *Why do you think of something so trivial at such a serious moment?*

Blow—head back—breathe; blow—head back—breathe. Where was the air going after it reached the unconscious man's lungs? Joe soon had his answer, and he took it for an encouraging sign. After Dave's lungs held all they could store, they reacted violently. Great bursts of bubbles shot periodically from his mouth. *Good,* Joe nodded in satisfaction. *His muscles are still able to contract.*

Each time Joe lifted his head, he monitored the activity going on around him. The nightmarish quality of movement was increasing with the futility every one of them felt. Mike was on the bank, pacing and yelling, "Dave, you can't die!" Was he going into shock?

Krys joined the crew still trying to move the rock. They were giving their all, holding nothing back. That was evident by their red and straining faces. But as far as Joe could see, the rock hadn't shifted at all.

Steve noticed a small come-a-long or hand winch lying discarded on the bank. He attached one end of the cable around an embedded rock, then tossed the other end to Andras, who dived down to secure it around the offending boulder. Steve grasped the ratchet handle firmly and jacked it up and down, hoping, of course, that each movement of the handle would tighten the cable and, inch by inch, would winch the boulder up onto the shore.

Unfortunately, the rock was not only massive, it was smooth. Four times they made the attempt, and four times the cable slipped off. They couldn't achieve the necessary "bite."

Andras suddenly had another idea. "Joe," he called, "what do you think about our heavy crowbar? I could hurry back to camp and get it."

Joe didn't answer. He heard the question, but he couldn't call up the necessary energy to respond. He knew Andras could never make it in time. Camp was simply too far.

Blow—head back—breathe; blow—head back—breathe. He had reached his own limit. His chest muscles went into a spasm of cramping with every deep breath.

"Mike, can you take over here?" he gasped.

Actually, Andras didn't wait for an answer from Joe. He climbed onto the bank and raced, dripping, all the way up the trail, across the bridge, down the other side and along the river until he reached the camp they'd left that morning.

Retracing his steps bearing the twenty-five-pound bar of steel, still at the same frantic rate of speed, his legs buckled like rubber but they continued to work. "Lucky it's been only six months since I skated the Danube (or Duna) River in winter, and swam across it each day during the months of summer," he panted. Even so—even considering his unusual state of physical fitness—running that distance rapidly after all he'd been through was a remarkable feat of endurance.

Mike worked above his cousin until he could no longer effectively function. Then Krys stepped in for a second turn.

Krys pressed the tips of his fingers against Dave's wrist. *There's no pulse!* The words screamed inside his head. Had he said them aloud? He felt again, willing himself to remain calm. *Definitely no pulse.*

His thoughts, so optimistic in the beginning, turned dark and ominous. *How is it possible for this man to die with so many of us here, doing everything in our power to save him? We can hold him in our hands; why can't we figure some way to get him out?* Then bitterly, *Why kid ourselves? He's dead! We may as well stop trying.*

He didn't articulate these negative emotions, even in the Polish that, with Andras missing at the time, only Joe could understand. The truth was that he had come to *care* what happened to this man whose voice he had never even heard. He thought of his own wife and three-year-old daughter waiting for him back home in Poland. What if the body under the rock were his?

He continued to do his best, knowing that in reality it would be a long time before he could bring himself to give up.

Bob Dorr stood on the river's edge, catching his breath. He knew that the man in the water had to have serious internal injuries. Once they got him out of the river, he would need more help than any of them could give him here in the hills. He raced off, going for the type of help only he could deliver.

He raced to his camper and turned on its CB radio. "Break one nine; break one nine." No answer. He smashed his fist against the dashboard in frustration. *My signal's not getting through! The cliffs must be blocking it!*

Shoving his truck roughly into gear, he roared up the road

to an open spot. An unidentified male voice answered immediately: "Hold on. I'll get the police!" His emergency call for help finally got out of the canyon.

For the first time since the accident, Mike felt the tiniest glimmer of hope. With someone else taking charge under the water, he was free to move around, to work on a new rescue angle.

He pushed himself upwards for the third time and restarted the engine on the dredger. *Dave's dead—he's got to be by now, but it's my responsibility to release his body and take it home.*

How long was it since he'd watched, in horror, as the boulder trapped his cousin under the surface of the water? Mike had no idea. He only knew that he was more grateful than he could hope to describe for the dedication of this many strangers and their selfless efforts to save his cousin's life.

Andras was back with the giant crowbar and he and Bob Ellis pried together against the rock.

Dropping down again, Mike scooped up the hose he'd abandoned at the first sound of danger and guided its powerful suction action underneath his cousin's hips.

The suction worked! That plus the heavy crowbar. By removing gravel from below and prying at the same time, they were eventually able to wriggle one leg free. And then the other. Joe slipped his hands under Dave's arms, Krys took his legs, and at last the whole limp body was carefully eased out from under the rock.

Joyce asked the question haunting everyone present: "Is there any chance at all that the underwater resuscitation attempt reached him in time?"

Dave wasn't breathing or exhibiting visible signs of life. His body was draped gently over gravel on the bank.

Now Krys definitely took charge. A sudden, fearful quiet enveloped the group, while Krys stood over the body shouting directions to Joe: "Pump him up. Pump him up while I take care of the CPR (cardiac pulmonary resuscitation). Hold his nose and pump his lungs three times by regular mouth-to-mouth. Don't allow any air to escape! I need the maximum capacity of air in his lungs to deliver full power CPR."

Joe assured him, "I understand. I'll do exactly as you instruct."

The whole process was repeated twice. Joe blew and Krys delivered powerful pressure on the chest to massage the heart. During the next set, with Joe's mouth still covering the dead man's, Dave vomited. Nauseated, Joe rolled away from him and threw up.

Dave's heart resumed beating and he started to gasp—short, rapid intakes intermingled with great wrenching shudders and bursts of bloody liquid spewing from his lips.

Krys jumped to his feet, shouting hysterically. "Zyje! Zyje! He's alive—alive! I was never so happy in my whole life as when I saw him take that first breath!" And dipping deep into a knowledge of English that nobody knew he possessed, he shouted "Lives—lives!" raising hands that trembled and with tears streaming unashamedly down his cheeks.

Fifteen minutes later fire and ambulance crews arrived. Dave suffered internal bleeding of undiagnosed intensity, and ambulance attendants were fearful his back or chest bones might be broken. They inched him onto a board for an "uncomfortable" ride to Auburn Faith Community Hospital. Dave pleaded weakly, "Slow down, you guys. And please—watch out for the bumps!"

He was kept in intensive care for two days of round-the-clock observation, tests, and treatment, while continuing to cough up substantial quantities of blood. Doctors were guarded in their prognosis, some doubting he would make it past that first afternoon. He was bruised so badly that nurses found it personally painful to insert the needle for an IV. They dreaded the bout with pneumonia doctors were convinced he still had to face.

Meanwhile, Dave ached all over. There wasn't a bone or muscle in his battered body that didn't scream with pain at the slightest movement.

While doctors labored to determine the extent of his injuries, Dave continued his own fight to survive. He and Laurie did a lot of praying those first few days in the hospital. Now he had time to concentrate on their baby and he didn't intend to go anywhere without making its acquaintance. (*His* acquaintance, as it turned out. His name is Bradley.)

Dave left the hospital still black and blue and hobbling on crutches, but alive. The pneumonia hadn't materialized.

Epilog

At that spot that has since come to be labeled the Death Hole, Dave was more fortunate than he or Mike immediately supposed. Underwater mouth-to-mouth resuscitation is an almost unknown form of first aid anywhere in the world, even among professionals trained in underwater rescue. The odds against a man knowledgeable in that procedure traveling from Poland to Los Angeles to the remote northern California hills, and then just happening to turn up at the exact time and place when his skills were needed, must be astronomical.

Incredibly, extensive hospital x-rays indicated that Dave came through the ordeal with no broken bones. He suspects his years of faithful soccer practice in high school and college and his overall athletic fitness might be partly responsible. His legs are unusually strong, with highly developed muscles. Still, the weight of the massive boulder should have crushed the strongest legs to jelly. Apparently, water-softened earth gave way and molded around him.

Now, after three years, he is almost completely recovered. The unusual method of resuscitation not only saved him at a time when his life was within seconds of slipping away, but did so without causing incapacitation of its own. His left hip still pains occasionally, mostly when he runs, and it pops sometimes when he moves it. Otherwise, he functions normally in every respect.

But his gold fever is entirely gone. Along with their dredging equipment. Mike and Dave were in *perfect* agreement about putting it all up for sale.

The prospect of wealth has given way completely to the greater goal of being around to raise his son.

"I learned something that day," Dave states solemnly. "Dredging for gold can be exciting, and the idea of striking it rich has a lot of appeal. But wealth isn't necessarily permanent—and families are forever!"

4

The End of the Story

The story behind Dave's near tragedy and how I became involved is almost as startling as the story itself.

I turned the key in my car's ignition at 10:45 A.M. on July 14, 1982, and along with the sound of the motor jumping to life I heard the crackle of the radio and the voice of a local news commentator winding up a late-breaking news flash:

". . . and has just been removed from the scene of the accident.

"In any case, it was a remarkable try. How often would a chance passerby in that remote, mountainous area be familiar with that unusual type of first aid—a

method most people have never heard of and would
never even think to attempt?"

Hearing only these scanty details, I was curious. What kind
of accident? What sort of first aid? Was the victim alive or
dead? I couldn't tell.

Two days later I was horrified to learn the extent of the
tragedy. The newsman hadn't been discussing bits and pieces
of a stranger's dilemma. He was speaking of Michael Astle, a
twenty-four-year-old friend of mine, and more specifically
about his cousin and closest friend, David Burgess.

Both are returned LDS missionaries. They don't claim a real
premonition of danger, but they do say that the eve of their
encounter with the boulder was the first time, of all the nights
they've spent in the wilds through the years, that they felt a
compelling need to kneel down together and pray for
protection out loud, family style. They always pray, night and
morning, but privately. Never before had their prayers been
offered jointly and out loud.

Two-and-a-half years later, I was compiling details of their
experience for this book when the letter came from *Reader's
Digest:* For their "Drama in Real Life" spot in the magazine,
would I look for a story with the same narrative suspense as
my chapter on suicide prevention they'd previously used?*
Needless to say, I would be delighted to try.

The further I delved into Mike and Dave's life-threatening
experience the more convinced I became that this story fit
the *Reader's Digest* outline exactly; and it had the added
benefit of containing unusual lifesaving information. I came
to feel strongly that everyone should be made aware that
underwater mouth-to-mouth resuscitation can be a practic-
able possibility in some circumstances.

*See Chapter 4 of the author's book, *No Greater Love* (Deseret Book
Company, 1982), and the March 1983 edition of *Reader's Digest*.

For the next two months I devoted all my time to research. The problem was that there was no way to track down witnesses to what I quickly discovered was an all but *unknown* type of first aid. In the confusion of removing Dave from the water and rushing him to the hospital, Mike hadn't written down names and addresses. Dave was unconscious during administration of the resuscitation, so it boiled down to Mike's word alone for proof of a procedure that several authorities told me probably couldn't have worked.

So I approached it from another angle. Surely somebody else, someplace in the world, was familiar with this procedure and could verify its effectiveness.

I spoke by telephone to people all over the country—to regional heads of the Red Cross, to a water safety expert at the YMCA, to professional scuba divers, to heads of swim schools. Even, in desperation, to the public information officer and the recently retired head of the President's Council on Physical Fitness in Washington, D.C.

Of all these people, *nobody* had heard of underwater mouth-to-mouth resuscitation. Several were excited with the idea and, having heard it described, felt sure it would do the job. The retired head of the President's Council said, "Bravo! Of course it would work. That's how most progress comes— not from the top, necessarily, but from someone down the line with enough ingenuity to try something new. I'm excited about having it made public!" But no one knew of anyone who had tried it.

I unearthed news about a novel made into a movie that dealt with such a concept, but it appeared to have no basis in fact.

I called a doctor in Canada who came from Czechoslovakia, and I questioned three visitors from Japan. Nothing.

Was it possible the procedure was widely known in Poland, perhaps? Not so! A Polish physics professor at a local university had likewise never heard of it. He kindly asked, "My dear, are you certain someone isn't pulling your leg?"

But I had the advantage of *knowing* it had worked. Dave was alive, sitting across the kitchen table from me, and Mike Astle—a young man I had known for years and trusted implicitly—was describing the action in detail.

But for my own peace of mind, and to get the information printed nationally, I knew I had to have substantiation. Especially for the *Reader's Digest.* Their research department takes each article line by line and verifies all the facts. Through weeks of research I'd spoken personally to probably three hundred ordinary people not involved in water safety, besides dozens of experts who are, and had reached dead ends at every turn.

The support system we have as Latter-day Saints is an awesome thing. It's always been my experience that if I try long enough, someone can be found through the vast Church network who is an expert on any subject one can imagine.

My visiting teachers dropped by. They commented that I looked tired. I was tired. Tired and discouraged. I'd spent all day on the phone, and the subject of underwater rescue was uppermost in my mind. I was thoroughly convinced by then that this story, if published, would not only entertain but could be a powerful instrument in saving who knows how many lives.

I could hardly believe it when Sharon Lee (my visiting teacher) said, "Oh, yes, I've heard of it. My daughter Shelley has done it. She learned it in a water safety class at Ricks College in Idaho."

I finished the article and sent it to *Reader's Digest.* They called to accept it, as excited by the possibilities as I was—except that they *needed* corroboration from the people who helped in the rescue. The *Reader's Digest* editor said, "Our research department gets very nervous about having people central to the plot whom they can't get their hands on." We ended the conversation with me promising to look again, to think and work on every possible angle, but having to frankly admit that locating even one participant seemed hopeless. I'd already tried.

We had almost no clues to go on. All we knew was that the man who did the actual resuscitation was Polish and came from Los Angeles; and that Dave had seen one of the miners before and that his first name was Steve. There was little possibility of turning those meager leads into living, breathing people.

I called Bill Hooper, who had dredged with Mike and Dave on previous occasions. I was grasping at straws. "Bill, isn't there *anything* you can tell me?" "Well, you might try that mining shop in Sacramento. (He wasn't even sure of the name, but he thought it began with the words *Mother Lode*.) Someone there might remember talk of an unusual rescue near Auburn two-and-a-half years ago. Sorry I can't be of more help!"

I searched the telephone book and located the mining shop. The owner referred me to his partner in Auburn. "Arnie would know about it if anybody would."

I called Arnie in Auburn. He remembered the situation, but details were foggy. He checked with three men in his shop. "Could the Steve you mention have been Steve Hagar? I'd ask him, but he's way back in the hills. That's rugged country. You can't reach him till he comes to town for supplies, and that might be weeks. I'm holding a miner's meeting tomorrow night, though. I'll ask around, and if anybody knows anything I'll call you Saturday morning."

Saturday morning came and went. No calls. Obviously Arnie hadn't made contact with the lost miners, or with anyone who could help me. I wasn't going to be able to furnish the corroboration the story required.

Saturday, noon. The phone rang. My heart nearly stopped beating when unfamiliar tones of a pleasant male voice said, "Kris Mackay? This is Steve Hagar. I understand you are looking for me."

So this is the end of the story. Encouragement given earlier by one of my good friends echoed again through my thoughts. Marilyn Drumright, one of the most spiritual women I know, had said: "Those witnesses aren't really lost. The Lord knows exactly where they are."

The smallest details came together miraculously. Steve had been the first one on the scene after Mike turned off the dredger and screamed for help, and he had names, addresses, and phone numbers of all the others. He could give them to me right now.

He hadn't intended to come to town that day. A sudden snowstorm in the mountains had forced him to leave the hills, keeping him conveniently stranded in Auburn long enough for me to visit him on Monday and get his angle of the story from his own lips. Using the numbers he furnished, I interviewed the others by phone, and later, most of them in person.

My next letter from *Reader's Digest* said, "That's an incredible piece of detective work—tracking down those sources of your gold-prospecting drama!" It was, and I'd love to consider myself the LDS Agatha Christie—but I can't take the credit. In essence, I stood by and watched—an eager spectator—while vital pieces of information fell into place around me. It was exciting!

Now I can't help wondering: *Why was it so important that this story be published?* Who will use underwater resuscitation months, or even years, down the road? Whose life might be saved? It would be fascinating to know.

5

The Gingerbread House

It's Christmastime as I write this.

Half a mile away, nestled off the road at the end of a private, winding lane, the two-story Huggins house is ablaze with light. Forty strings of tiny, colored bulbs twinkle brightly through a grove of trees that separates the property from the street. They outline every doorway and window, porch or eave, every nook and cranny of an intriguing structure that could easily pass for a magical gingerbread house from pages of a storybook.

Bringing the house to life with lights each holiday season was a tradition long before the Huggins family bought the property. And implicit in the sales contract was their promise that the custom would be continued.

Basking in its glow, one feels it might be the last house on earth whose occupants would cower in fear within its fabled walls. But that's the way it was.

In the mid-nineteen-seventies, our county was held in the paralyzing grip of a madman known as the East Area Rapist. He crept into homes secretly in the dead of night, often through an unlocked patio door or a window opened an inch or two for ventilation.

In the beginning he was only a shadowy figure we read about in our morning newspaper. We shivered over published accounts of his intrusions, but at first they hardly seemed real. Unfortunately he struck viciously and often, and soon most of us knew one of his victims—or were acquainted with a friend-of-a-friend who knew one—and we saw firsthand the suffering caused by his nocturnal visits.

His was the type of unspeakable crime that affects all of us. Perhaps *most* devastating was that he struck in places we like to think of as havens from the cruelty of the world—our homes—and there seemed to be no practical or certain defense.

He craved publicity, and he left behind distinctive evidence of his presence. Police, wary of copycats, withheld news of most of his strange and cowardly practices. All we of the general public knew for sure was that the intruder wore a ski mask to hide his facial features, and when a man was found sleeping in the home, that man was roused from sleep at gun- or knife-point. He was tied up on hands and knees with a cup and saucer balanced delicately on his back. In case of any movement whatsoever—any straining at the bonds that bound him—the china would rattle, alerting the attacker to more drastic action that had already been graphically described to the potential victim.

The man of the house was thus stripped of power to even try to protect his home, and that proved to be as emotionally damaging to him as the attack on his wife or daughter was to her.

Needless to say, each girl or woman in the area—and every husband and father—lived in constant dread that their house might be targeted next.

The first hint that someone had violated *their* privacy surfaced as Roy Huggins reached under the mattress for his gun. Roy is a sheriff's deputy. After work he habitually pushed his revolver into the middle of their king-sized bed, secreted between the mattress and the springs. He consciously shoved it far enough from the edge so that the short arms of seven-year-old Jason could never reach it. He felt again. The gun had to be there! Where could it have gone?

He called Judy and together they stripped the bed of its covers and mattress. No revolver.

They tiptoed into the adjoining room where Jason lay asleep. Might he have wiggled his whole little body beneath the mattress to find his daddy's gun? If so, where would he put it?

Carefully they checked around his sleeping body. They removed the blankets one by one. They slipped their hands under *his* mattress until both were convinced it wasn't there.

Roy felt the first real stirrings of uneasiness. He was aware there would have been time for a stranger to slip into the house and remove the gun. The Huggins family owned a small neighborhood grocery. After work in his patrol car, Roy always stopped at home to drop off his revolver and slip out of uniform before working an hour or two at the store.

He ran downstairs for a quick search of the premises. On the floor outside of the bathroom lay his empty holster, and a foot or so away, a spool of white medical tape that clearly didn't belong in their home. His heart beat faster.

He was a policeman and consequently was familiar with details of the East Area Rapist's activities. Pieces of the puzzle began to fall into place. Now he was scared, but he didn't want to communicate the extent of those fears to his wife. Not quite yet.

He summoned friends on the force and they dusted for fingerprints. They checked the grounds. Someone had left footprints on moist ground at the east side of the house, then climbed the outside of the fireplace, stepped over to the air conditioner, and gained access to their home through a window in Jason's bedroom. That route of entry involved a fair amount of physical dexterity. Roy's throat tightened even more. The East Area Rapist was known to be athletic.

Other policemen came, and they asked specific questions, some of which made no sense at all to Judy. She understood their request to thoroughly check her jewelry, and it appeared that nothing was missing. What she found confusing was their insistence that she make sure no photographs were missing. She checked and double-checked. They weren't satisfied. Wasn't there a spot somewhere in the house with a photo album she had forgotten?

There was! Her wedding album was stored in a chest upstairs. She hadn't looked at it for years. But turning the pages, with policemen looking over her shoulder, she was startled to find a page that was empty. Discoloration of the paper pointed to the spot where a picture had previously lain.

Now she had to be warned. They had no choice. Every clue unearthed in the Huggins home was typical of the East Area Rapist's method of operation. He gained access to a house in advance, picked up a picture of his intended victim (among other things), and slipped away undetected. Usually it was in the neighborhood of two weeks later when he returned.

Now an alarm system was installed in their attic. Wires were placed under rugs surrounding their bed. The touch of a toe on one of those rugs would instantly sound the alarm. Deadbolt locks were attached to doors, and windows were made doubly secure.

In effect, the storybook Huggins home was turned into a jail, and the Huggins family—especially Judy—became its prisoners.

She was escorted to work at the bank every morning with a loaded gun ready in her purse and was instructed to meet her husband at the grocery store before daring to return home at night. Shopping alone at any time was off limits, as was any kind of activity that normally makes life worthwhile. She was forbidden to step out into her yard. Once locked inside the house, Judy must never, never open her door to anyone, unless Roy or some other officer was present.

It was a life more draining than she could have imagined, and it quickly took its toll. With nerves frayed beyond belief, they forfeited all semblance to family life that once they had taken for granted. Judy heard herself snapping at her son: "Don't you dare touch that door!" Jason grew progressively more white and drawn, and more often than not was in tears. Their waking hours revolved totally around the need to shut themselves away, and they dreamed of danger as they slept.

The time arrived when Judy couldn't live this way any longer. It was degrading. She was a daughter of her Heavenly Father, and as such she was entitled to some measure of dignity. And so were Jason and Roy.

She begged Roy to arrange for removal of the stifling protection. Two indescribable months had elapsed. Surely authorities didn't suppose that that maniac was still coming back!

Roy did speak to the authorities and was assured that the alarm probably was no longer functional. The batteries would have gone dead by then. "Don't worry about it. We'll stop by one of these days to pick up our equipment." In reality they weren't ready to risk removal of the system.

A week later Roy needed an extra electrical extension cord. He'd lent his to the workmen installing the alarm because one of their cords hadn't operated correctly. He hesitated before removing it from the intricate tangle of plugs and wires, but after all, the batteries were dead and the cord *did* belong to him.

Almost before his hand left the cord, four green and white patrol cars screamed down their private lane and screeched to a halt in their driveway. Sirens blared and car doors were left swinging as officers pointed drawn guns at the house.

The batteries weren't dead after all. When the alarm sounded at the fire station at the touch of Roy's hand on the cord, attendants monitoring it swung into action. Immediately they called the bank. Sorry, Judy wasn't there. Where was she? She'd gone home for lunch.

Judy simply couldn't continue under these restrictions. The time had arrived when she was even more frightened about what the tension was doing to her family than she was of the rapist.

She had earnestly prayed for protection during those impossible months, and now she was prepared to *insist* that their lives return to normal. Foolish, perhaps, when judged from the coldly clinical viewpoint of the world. But the world doesn't take into account the still, small voice. Somehow Judy knew then that, trusting in her Heavenly Father, she and her loved ones had no need to fear.

Nobody claims that Judy's prayers alone put an end to the grip of terror in our area. Surely thousands of prayers must have joined together in their flight toward heaven, and surely every one of them was heard.

But from that time on, the East Area Rapist dropped abruptly out of sight. Gradually, as weeks grew into months without our reading of another attack, all of us relaxed.

Police are convinced he moved his operations to a neighboring community. There, in the process of a similar crime that exactly matched secret methods of *our* assailant, an intruder in a ski mask was shot and fatally wounded.

Apparently his fame had spread, and someone had grimly prepared for his coming.

This story ends with an unusual twist. Judy had already received protection, even before she realized she needed it.

Several months after her decision to trust her safety to the power of the Lord, she learned it hadn't been the East Area Rapist who violated the privacy of her home. It was, in fact, a sixteen-year-old neighbor she and her husband had befriended. He was a young man, large in stature and athletic, whose background held skirmishes of various sorts with the law, some far more serious than they had suspected.

He became close to the family. He worked part-time in their store, and even rode in the patrol car with Roy on occasion, or visited police headquarters in his company. Overhearing bits of conversations between officers, he pieced together unpublished activities of the rapist. Cursed with a hair-trigger temper, one day he decided to punish the Huggins family for some imagined slight from Roy by recreating the dreaded scene exactly.

Judy entered their house alone on the day he stole the gun. She passed within inches of the closed bathroom door behind which he was hiding, desperately afraid he would be caught with a stolen, loaded gun and sent to juvenile prison (which he later was).

She noticed the door was closed, and thought briefly of flipping it open as she passed, but she was in a hurry to get to their store. Jason was in the garage, and her grandmother waited outside in the car. They'd stopped by the house only long enough to turn on the Christmas lights because visitors would drive by from miles away, and she didn't want them disappointed.

Judy was left with a lasting impression of the value of listening to the Spirit. Sometimes waking with a start in the middle of the night, she wonders what might have happened if she'd opened up that door.

6

The Daughter and Her Dad

Judy Stoeltzing delivered the eulogy at her father's funeral.

She was an only child, accustomed through the years to filling dual roles as her parents' only daughter *and* only son. Funerals are emotional occasions at best, and delivering his eulogy was the hardest task she'd ever appointed herself to tackle. But she had something special she wanted to tell him.

Judy and her husband were recent converts to Mormonism. It weighed heavily on their souls that there hadn't been an opportunity to teach her busy father the gospel. Even at the end there wasn't time. His leaving came about so suddenly. He was driven to the hospital on Sunday, and by Monday evening he was gone.

She missed him terribly already. Her son Jimmy wasn't the only member of the family who felt a numbing void at his absence.* They all did.

So at the funeral Judy spoke directly to the father who (among other accomplishments) had interviewed Eleanor Roosevelt as a Washington, D.C., newspaper correspondent and had traveled up dense, steamy jungles along the Amazon River searching out rubber plantations for a United States rubber company. Charles Carroll Miller—named after one of the signers of the Declaration of Independence—was a man who had done more in his sixty-six years than most could cram into several lifetimes.

In the eulogy she reminded him that life had taken him on a worldwide, relentless search for knowledge of all kinds. His was a nose for news that was eternal. Now he was finally in the perfect spot to uncover the greatest news story of all time.

Assuming that by now he must know the basic, fundamental facts—that God is really God and Jesus is indeed the Christ—she charged him not to rest until he dug out the rest of the story. She promised him enough lead time that he could finish and be ready before his temple work was begun. But he must act swiftly; she didn't intend to delay indefinitely.

Two years later Judy sat in the serene, pale green assembly room of the Oakland Temple. She had kept her end of the agreement and today was the day. She felt good about her father's proxy. Austin G. Hunt, stake patriarch, was the father of one of her closest friends and a man within a year of the age her father would have been.

She was happy with Brother Hunt's delight in performing this act of kindness for her father, but her thoughts centered

---

*See Chapter 10 of the author's book, *The Outstretched Arms* (Bookcraft, 1983).

mostly on her dad and his possible attitude. Was he ready? Had she given him enough time?

The session was ready to begin. Participants clothed in white were settled comfortably in their seats, and the doors to the hall had been closed.

Judy looked around. The spacious room was hushed, each mind being occupied in its owner's own brand of quiet meditation. That hallowed place seemed to Judy to hover halfway between heaven and earth, not belonging to either world exclusively but a vital part of both.

She glanced up casually at the empty expanse of wall ahead of her. Empty? Not quite! Three radiant yet indistinct figures moved against the right lower corner of the wall, resembling actors in an old, faded movie, on-screen in a theater which hasn't been properly darkened.

She looked more closely. The figures were clearly men in temple clothing. One man stood slightly in front of the other two, who flanked him on either side and appeared to be escorting the first man to a place of honor.

She strained to make out the man's facial features. The light surrounding them was too brilliant, but everything about his bearing and manner caused her to inwardly cry out, "That man is my father!" Then the figures passed out of her sight.

Almost in shock, she let her eyes leave the wall and quickly scanned the room. There was no change in the quiet contemplation of those around her. The vision that had been so clear to her had been opened to her eyes alone.

Judy never visits the temple now without remembering the day when her father came to accept his work in person and for a few glorious seconds the veil separating them disappeared.

7

The Insurmountable Problem
(Part 1)

Dr. Randolph Mitchell,* general practitioner/surgeon, seemed to have it all. He was happily married to a wonderful woman, had four fine sons, lived in a beautiful and well-run home, and had a lucrative practice and devoted patients. He was also possessed of a delightful laugh and an extraordinarily magnetic personality. People loved him wherever he went.

Yes, Randy had it all—including an apparently insurmountable problem.

Although raised in a strong home by goodly parents, he'd fallen into the trap of idolizing a school professor who was agnostic, one who didn't hesitate stressing that fact in his

---

*Not his real name.

lectures. The professor didn't believe in the existence of God or in other "religious claptrap," and before young Randy left that sphere of influence he was confused.

As is often the case when religious persons turn away from truth, Randy couldn't seem to leave it alone. He was a born tease, and at family gatherings he delighted in pushing all he now found lacking in religion per se and in chiding his brothers and sisters for being foolish enough to believe. It was almost as if subconsciously he sought to hear the one rebuttal he wouldn't be able to refute.

Randy's confusion was hard on his family and especially painful for his remarkably spiritual mother, who loved him dearly. She was unusually close to the Lord, and knew with an almost perfect knowledge the spiritual dangers swirling about her son. She constantly prayed in his behalf. Every night and morning she beseeched God to help her son see clearly once again; specifically, to send into his life some dramatic experience that would impress him.

Several years slipped uneventfully by. Dr. Mitchell's practice thrived. His patients clearly adored him, particularly the older people, who were bolstered as much by his loving concern and compassion as by the medication he prescribed.

One afternoon Randy and an elderly patient emerged from a treatment room, both cackling with laughter. The woman steadied herself on one corner of the desk while she caught her breath and wiped her eyes, and she chuckled, "Dr. Mitchell, I don't remember exactly what ailment brought me in here, but I sure do feel better now!"

So life went on without change while his mother continued to pray.

One day Randy and another doctor, a colleague, worked feverishly at the bedside of a dying young woman. Her husband and children waited tensely outside the door.

She did pass away. The two physicians examined her carefully, pronounced her dead, and turned to leave the room.

But as they neared the door, the woman began to speak. In a voice heavy with awe, she murmured, "How beautiful it is here!" and "How wonderful to see you again!"—obviously speaking to loved ones on the other side.

Dr. Mitchell stiffened, then whirled around. As she continued to speak, he sensed that a multitude of unseen spirits were with them in the room. Almost paralyzed with shock, he forced his resisting body to move toward her bed. He knew it was impossible, but now she was breathing!

She opened her eyes, looked directly into his, and whispered, "Dr. Mitchell, call my family in. Hurry! I don't have much time."

For the next few glorious moments he was a witness to the most humbling experience of his life. He listened spellbound while the woman explained to her husband and children that, much as she loved them, she had been in a world so beautiful that she longed to return. She begged them not to grieve. Understanding how devastated they would be at her passing, she had asked for, and somehow been granted, a few short moments to help them accept the purpose of her leaving. She stressed again how deeply she loved them. But where she was going, she truly wanted to be.

Who can say what prompted her brief return? Was it solely to comfort her family? Or was it partly a merciful Father's answer to a beloved daughter's unwavering prayers for her son? Or a combination of both?

Whatever the purpose, it did comfort her family, and it also profoundly affected the man who had been led in his formative years to doubt the very existence of God and his realm.

For days Randy couldn't eat or sleep. I was his sister's visiting teacher, and I heard his story in detail as it unfolded. It happened twenty years ago, while our children were still toddlers.

Randy retreated alone into his bedroom and locked the door

even to his wife. In those concentrated hours of stunned soul-searching that followed, his submerged testimony resurfaced. Now he *believed,* and he worshipped his newly found Savior with all his heart. Never again would he bait his brothers and sisters with religious versus scientific traps.

It appeared his mother's prayers had all been answered. But in Randy's case it wasn't quite that easy . . .

8

The Insurmountable Problem
(Part 2)

What, in the long run, constitutes real, true, *legitimate* tragedy? How widely does the broad, celestialized viewpoint differ from our narrow, mortal perception?

In Dr. Randolph Mitchell's case it would be nice to report that his entire life-style underwent a dramatic transformation when his testimony of God resurfaced. Unfortunately, it wasn't that easy.

Believing as he previously had—or rather, being confused and not sure of what he *did* believe—or perhaps because of his likeable, easygoing personality, he'd drifted into the habit of partying, and he found he enjoyed drinking. It was relaxing. The study and practice of medicine is long, hard, tedious work. Why not take a glass or two with friends from time to time?

And so he did, unaware that he was one of those unfortunates who becomes easily and powerfully addicted and thus turn over control of a portion of their lives to a force outside themselves. He didn't realize how insidious its hold on him was until he attempted to give it up. But by then, drinking was an established part of his routine.

Now, though his mind and heart were strengthened, the stranglehold of physical addiction remained. He battled it ferociously and made noticeable gains, but he was never able to sustain them. One moment of weakness undid days and weeks of hard-won strength.

The problem was that his day-to-day pattern of living hadn't been altered. The long, exhausting hours of draining concern he put into his practice, old friends who urged him to stop on the way home for just one drink, and his legitimate need for relaxation—all were still there pulling at him in vulnerable moments. In spite of heroic efforts and fierce determination he couldn't shake the old habits.

His drinking never interfered with the calibre of treatment offered to his patients. It was tucked unobtrusively but with frightening compulsion into the few hours he allowed himself away from the hospital.

His children grew up strong in the faith with the help of their father's wise counsel, and in the beginning he was instrumental in converting his nonmember wife. But there were times without number when he was in no condition to take his place as head of the household.

No, his patients were not shortchanged. Only he and his family knew what this life-style cost him in terms of daily suffering and of family or spiritual opportunities missed.

As years continued to tick away it become harder and harder for him to reconcile his by-now pervasive beliefs with this compulsive behavior, and he put up valiant, recurring struggles to conquer it. When he couldn't, his conscience suffered tremendously.

One morning in early 1966, the eldest Mitchell boy approached his father. He was nearing missionary age, and the thing he desired more than anything in the world was to enter the temple for the first time with both his father and mother at his side.

Randy wanted that too, desperately. One final time, this time with more motivation than ever before, he worked to turn his life around, to prepare himself to be worthy to take his family to the house of the Lord.

It still wasn't easy. It was the hardest battle he'd ever waged. But this time he succeeded. He met his goal, and the Mitchell family was sealed in the Manti Temple for time and all eternity on March 3, 1967. They made eternal and serious vows. Now their prayers were prayers of thanksgiving.

Four months later, however, subtle, unnerving signs indicated to Randy that his struggle wasn't all behind him as he had confidently supposed. Apparently it would hound him as a life-long, touch-and-go affair—a mortal battle every step of the way to keep under control the addiction he'd embraced so casually in his youth.

Randy continued to spend long hours on his knees in a desperate effort to hold his enemy at bay. During one such period his mother happened to visit in their home. He took her aside and begged, "Mother, I know how much the Lord loves you. Will you please come with me into the bedroom to pray?"

So on their knees together they pleaded that Randy might be given strength to match his desire. They solemnly reminded their Father of his promise in 1 Corinthians not to allow a burden greater than his children could bear: "God . . . will not suffer you to be tempted above that ye are able; but will with the temptation also make a way to escape" (1 Corinthians 10:13).

Randy, Susan, and their sons drove to Lake Almanor for a rare, short vacation. Susan and the boys took in a movie that first evening, leaving an exhausted Randy in the cabin alone to rest.

They returned from the movie to find his body slumped over the table. An autopsy confirmed that he'd choked on possibly the one food that even a doctor, alone, wouldn't be able to expel—the peanut butter and crackers still clutched in his hand.

So what *is* tragedy? Certainly the Lord does not look on death as we do. Death is a fact of life which must be faced and ultimately experienced by all who are born into mortality. The timing is what counts.

Randy's griefstricken family found themselves comforted in their loss. His ordeal was over. He went while living principles he'd struggled a good portion of his adult life to be able to sustain.

To their sorrowing minds, a compassionate Father took into account the overwhelming desires of Randy's heart, recognized his eternal worth, and lovingly allowed him to come home.

9

Miss Tomoko Iida

Picture a country so densely populated that seventy million people live in an area smaller than the state of California—a country so crowded that major railway terminals employ safety guards at rush hour to push the passengers inside.

Seats on Japan's famous Shinkansen or "bullet train" are reserved, but not so on the commuters. A train thunders into a station in Tokyo every few seconds, for example, and in less than a minute thousands of passengers pour into the seats and fill every available inch of footspace. A few, unable in the crush of humanity to make it all the way inside on their own, find that some part of their anatomy still protrudes through the opening. Hence the safety guards and their unique method of closing the bulging doors.

Japan's railway system probably is the finest and fastest in the world. The bullet train didn't get its affectionate nickname by dawdling along the tracks.

The Church of Jesus Christ of Latter-day Saints is meeting with great success in Japan. But considering the sheer numbers of people who live on those islands, plus the almost unbelievable difficulty my husband and I had in locating the Yokohama chapel, it was clear that much proselyting remains to be done before most Japanese citizens even suspect we Mormons exist.

My husband's employment takes him all over the world and I go with him when I can. In May 1983 he went to Japan for three fast-paced weeks and I happily tagged right along. We headquartered in Yokohama, with side trips to a satisfying number of other interesting cities.

It's fascinating to see how other people live. Perhaps it's especially intriguing in the Orient, where life-styles are so different from our own—the food, the customs, the tiny delicacy of the people (who try not to stare as we tower above them at my husband's awesome six foot four and my "ordinary" five foot six).

A number of Japanese people do speak English, but even more of them don't. Invariably polite and helpful, nevertheless our congenial hosts found occasions when they were hard put to figure out what on earth it was we wanted.

Like the Sunday we tried to locate a Latter-day Saint building.

Our hotel clerk repeated quizzically, "Mor-mon? *Mor-mon?*" It wasn't until he produced an English telephone book that we were able to make him understand, and even then it wasn't easy. Thanks to his willingness to keep trying and the taxi driver's congeniality in stopping twice to telephone for further instructions, we eventually arrived in time for the meeting.

A pervading Japanese national characteristic is formal politeness. They smile a lot, even laugh behind a modestly upraised hand that covers the mouth, but one is never certain what they *feel*. Inscrutable might be an appropriate word to describe them. They are gracious and friendly without revealing innermost thoughts for fear of being considered forward or rude.

Miss Tomoko Iida is like that. She's tiny and delicate, a typically lovely girl in her early twenties. She dropped by our hotel in the town of Meto to show us the sights.

Normally, she isn't a guide. She holds a management position with a manufacturing firm, but because her English is fluent she was nominated to show us the local shogun castle with its famous and sculptured grounds.

She arrived at our Japanese-style hotel with two limousines. On that day we traveled with Greg and Maria Rowsey, an American business colleague of my husband's and his new and very young bride. The Rowseys are wonderful companions. They were currently celebrating their honeymoon with a two-year work excursion in Japan. Not thinking it polite to crowd the four of us into only one car, Miss Iida thoughtfully brought two.

Ed and I were not surprised when she climbed into the other limousine with Greg and Maria. The three of them were closer to the same general age. Later on, strolling among exotic trees in the castle gardens, she drifted closer to us and a friendship of some warmth began to develop.

Of course we were pleased to have her function almost as our personal and private escort, because she acquainted us with details we otherwise would have missed. For instance, the floors of the castle—nightingale floors—have a birdlike, musical squeak. No matter how carefully we placed our stockinged feet we couldn't avoid that sound of chirping. Without Miss Iida in close attendance we wouldn't have known they were constructed in that fashion deliberately.

Enemies of the early shogun were everywhere, but thanks to the floors they couldn't slip up behind him unnoticed!

The afternoon flew by and at last our tour time was spent. The park closed and Miss Iida, glancing at her watch, informed us cordially that she must now escort us to the banquet planned for us that evening.

This time we weren't surprised when she joined us in *our* limousine for the return trip. By then we were relaxed and comfortable with each other, though still extremely formal in our speech.

Our driver spoke no English at all. He drove without a word from his position on the right. (I hadn't been aware that, like the English, Japanese drivers steer from what we Americans label the passenger side.) Miss Iida joined him on the left.

We chatted at random as the miles passed swiftly under our wheels. The drive took half an hour. Miss Iida mentioned pleasantly that she looked forward to a visit to the United States someday. She was saving money and by the end of two years should have enough set aside to manage the trip. Moreover, she had pen pals in America. Making casual conversation to pass the time, Ed asked where the pen pals lived. She named New York, California, Utah, Alaska . . .

"Utah? My wife and I both came from Utah. I was born in Salt Lake City and she was born in Ogden."

Miss Iida grew very still for a moment. She almost stopped breathing. Then she asked in a tiny, breathless voice, "Are you *Mormons,* by any chance?"

When Ed confirmed that we are, her mask of inscrutability shattered. Tears welled up in her eyes, then spilled over and ran profusely down her cheeks.

Turning completely around she perched on her knees and reached across the back of the seat to fling her arms toward us in an uncharacteristically impulsive gesture. Grasping my two hands with her left hand and Ed's in her right, she sobbed, "Oh, Brother Mackay! Sister Mackay! I am Mormon, too!"

For a moment we were stunned. Then all traces of formality between us evaporated. Suddenly we were brother and sisters in a land where Latter-day Saints are still only a tiny fraction of a minority, with a bond of love that none of us had dreamed we commonly shared. How easily we could have met and parted without experiencing that precious moment!

My first thought was, "How grateful I am that she liked us before she knew who we are." Ed and I each said a private little prayer of thanksgiving that we three were irresistably drawn to each other with that invisible, mysterious *something* before we realized we were spiritual kin.

What thoughts occupied the driver's mind during this unusual exchange we can't begin to imagine. He didn't turn a hair. With eyes straight ahead and no change of expression, he continued to drive down the road.

Miss Iida—Tomoko by now—tearfully filled us in on her story. She was converted and baptized two years earlier, away at school. When she returned to live at her parents' home, they forbade her to mingle with her beloved Saints or to attend LDS services. They were Buddhists—good people, but they couldn't allow her to attend a "foreigners'" church. Through her sobs she assured us, "But I want you to know that I pray every night and that's why I'm saving to move to the United States."

We clung to each other and cried together as we offered her words of encouragement and strength. We implored her to hang on to her ideals and assured her the way would open up for her to live the life she desired.

By then we were approaching the banquet hall. Our car turned down the long, graceful driveway that winds past a sparkling fishpond and a Buddhist shrine, and the mask descended once more. Her last words to us as *Sister* Iida were, "Please don't tell anyone at my company what I've just revealed to you. I'm afraid I would be fired if they suspected I am a Christian!" With that statement she carefully dried her tears and arranged her face so that it became the formal Miss Iida we had originally met.

She guided us into the banquet room, where a long table on the floor was deliciously set with dishes calculated to introduce us to the best of their country's hospitality.

I was quickly absorbed in conversation with two of our hosts and didn't notice that she planned to leave. Ed touched my elbow and whispered, "Kris, Miss Iida is waiting to tell you good-bye."

I turned to face her, and in tones of polite friendliness such as one pleasant stranger would use with another we exchanged farewells. We shook hands and bowed, and Miss Iida said with her trace of enchanting accent, "Good-bye, Mrs. Mackay. It was so nice to meet you. I hope to see you again someday." Ed and I knew what she meant, and we're positive that she knew that we knew.

We have written often since then. Her first letter waited when we reached home in America, and it said: "I believe Heavenly Father allowed us to meet. He knew how alone I felt and how badly I needed your strength."

As for Ed and me, we saw unusual, exciting things on that trip to the Orient, more than we could possibly describe. But our meeting with Tomoko Iida and the love we briefly shared—a love we expect to last for all eternity—was the undisputed highlight of them all.

10

The Cross-Country Flight

"Mr. Palmer? Mr. Dennis Palmer?"

"I'm Dennis Palmer."

Dennis looked up into the smiling eyes of a stewardess as she moved toward him down the aisle, holding in her hand what appeared to be some kind of passenger manifest. He flies often, and this was one more important cross-country business trip.

He was a little puzzled. Funny. He'd never before been asked to identify himself *after* boarding a flight. Must be something new.

The plane still sat on the ground at the Long Beach airport, but Dennis had already removed papers from a briefcase for his presentation in Chicago that afternoon and they were spread out across his lap. He planned to occupy himself during the flight with last-minute study.

The attractive young woman smiled again. Undoubtedly stewardesses are chosen partly for their ability to put passengers at ease.

"Do you live in California, Mr. Palmer? Were you born here?"

"I live in Orange County, but originally I came from Idaho."

"Have you ever been back East, say—to New York?"

"Yes, I have, as a matter of fact. I spent two years on the East Coast on a mission for my church, but that was a long time ago. Twelve years ago, at least."

The young woman rested her elbow against the seat in front of him, and leaned foward. "How interesting! Are you LDS?"

Just then the pilot started the plane's engines, and the stewardess stepped backwards, explaining hurriedly that she had preflight duties to complete. "After I'm finished I'll come back and talk to you again, if you don't mind."

Dennis watched her walk gracefully up the aisle, pausing to check a loose seat belt on the left or to give a final word of instruction to a novice traveler on the right. Then he pulled his attention back to the papers waiting on his lap.

Suddenly he realized he wasn't thinking of the facts and figures typed neatly on those pages. Though his eyes were dutifully scanning each line, his mind was elsewhere. Mention of his mission had sent his thoughts winging across the miles well ahead of the plane. In memory he was back in New York, living in a well-to-do suburb of Rochester where he and his companion rented a room with kitchen privileges. The few months spent in that area still bothered him. The trouble was that in spite of earnest and dedicated efforts he was afraid he hadn't accomplished anything really worthwhile.

They weren't accepted by their neighbors. True, most were congenial and spoke in passing, but these people were self-sufficient, able to take care of themselves. They felt no need for religious instruction.

The Elders contacted houses in the immediate vicinity and then moved on to tracting two or three miles away from home.

Neighborhood children were the bright spot of their day. Returning home in the evenings they were greeted with squeals of delight and nearly always stopped a minute to throw a football, play a game, or just tease one of the boys or girls good-naturedly as they would a younger brother or sister. Both were from large families, and their interaction with children filled a void in their lives at that time.

Eating lunch one day, they smiled, listening to sounds of fun in an adjoining yard. But abruptly the shouts of playing changed to screams of agony. The Elders dropped their sandwiches and bolted out of the door.

They ran to the backyard of the house next door and absorbed the grisly scene in one terrible glance. One young friend—a girl about six years old—lay screaming hysterically on the grass. She'd been sliding on a long, plastic slide coated by a stream of water from the hose, while her brother cut the lawn. Somehow she had slid into the mower. One portion of her tiny foot—from arch to upper heel—had been completely severed.

The girl's mother stood frozen in horror. Frantic, screaming children ran around in circles or raced out of the yard, unable to cope with the shock that confronted their eyes.

Blood poured from the ghastly wound. The Elders scooped up a towel that lay on the lawn by the slide and tore it in halves. Kneeling quickly at her side, they applied a tourniquet to her leg. She wouldn't last long if blood continued to escape at the rate it was going. Her mother ran inside for clean towels as the Elders administered a hasty blessing to the girl. One of them carried a key chain containing a small vial of consecrated oil.

The mother returned with fresh towels and they wrapped

the injured foot securely. This was 1969. Reattachment of severed limbs was a fairly new process at that time. They picked up her mangled heel, gathered the little girl up in their arms, and started at once to get help. Fortunately an emergency facility was located only blocks from the house.

Doctors worked on her immediately. Elder Palmer and his companion waited tensely outside in the hallway. Before long the mother stepped out of the treatment room and into the hall. Looking at them with haggard eyes, she begged, "Will you come in and pray for my daughter?"

It's unusual to administer a second blessing within minutes of the first, but both felt that doing so would in this case be proper procedure. The mother wasn't present during the first one, and since she had asked for their help, they felt strongly impressed to offer her some form of tangible spiritual consolation.

A doctor worked at her feet while they put their hands on her head and promised, by the authority they held to act in God's name, that she would recover, that she would regain full use of her foot and suffer no permanent side effects—that she would be able to live a full and normal life and would walk without a limp.

As they spoke they were aware that the doctor stopped working. They left the room and he followed. He caught up to them in the hall.

He scowled. "How dare you hold out that ridiculous hope? Don't you realize that girl's Achilles' tendon has been severed? The main tendon that connects to the calf of the leg and affects movement of her whole little foot? She will require months or years of surgery and therapy. Possibly she will walk again—someday—but I doubt it. If she does, most assuredly it *won't* be without a limp!"

The missionaries left the hospital with the doctor's angry words ringing in their ears. A trifle discouraged, perhaps, but not wholly. They were convinced they had acted under a direction that superseded the doctor's.

Soon after that incident they were pulled out of the area and that part of the mission was closed. No other Elders took their place. They went on to other cities and were shortly involved in more productive work.

Three months later Elder Palmer and his new companion attended the Hill Cumorah pageant. Someone called his name, and glancing around he saw the little girl from Rochester. A cast covered the full length of her leg, and attempting to hurry to speak to him before the pageant started, she came, of course, with a *decided* limp. He didn't see her parents. Thousands of spectators sat at the foot of the hill. The pageant began, and after it was over their paths didn't cross.

Elder Palmer's mission was over. Before he left for home he stopped at mission headquarters and filled out a referral card in the name of the injured girl's parents.

His life from then on followed a typical returned-missionary pattern. He returned to school at Brigham Young University, graduated, married, moved to Southern California, and embarked on his career in business. His life was going well. But sometimes—like today—he couldn't help wondering about that little girl. . .

He was pulled from his reverie by the touch of a hand on his shoulder. The stewardess had come back and was speaking.

"You don't remember me, do you?" she laughed.

He looked at her closely. "No, I'm sorry. I don't. Have we met someplace before?"

She was—you may have already guessed—the little girl the doctor doubted would ever use her foot normally—walking without a trace of a limp and working in an occupation noted for seeking physical perfection in its employees. Missionaries had visited her family in response to the referral card, and all of their lives had been altered. Her father was a member of the high council; her mother was active in the ward Relief Society presidency; and her brother was currently on a mission.

As for the girl herself, she remembered that Elder Palmer came from somewhere in the west, and she searched for him on every flight. She wanted him to know that in less than a month she would be married in the Washington Temple.

When the plane landed in Chicago, Dennis almost floated off. He hardly needed to use the stairs.

This had been a memorable flight.

11

Tolstoy and Warner

"Dr. White, said Count Tolstoi, "I wish you would tell me about your American religion."

"We have no state church in America," replied Dr. White. . . .[Andrew D. White, former president of Cornell University and at this time United States Ambassador to Germany, was relating to Thomas J. Yates an experience he had had with Count Leo Tolstoi while serving as United States Foreign Minister to Russia in 1892.]

Then Count Leo Tolstoi, in his honest and stern, but lovable, manner, rebuked the ambassador. "Dr. White, I am greatly surprised and disappointed that a man of your great learning and position should be so ignorant on this important subject. The Mormon people teach

the American religion; their principles teach the people not only of Heaven and its attendant glories, but how to live so that their social and economic relations with each other are placed on a sound basis....
If Mormonism is able to endure, unmodified, until it reaches the third and fourth generation, it is destined to become the greatest power the world has ever known." (Quoted in LeGrand Richards, *A Marvelous Work and a Wonder* [Deseret Book Company, 1976], pp. 413-14.)

Dale Warner stood, fascinated, in the hallway of Count Leo Tolstoy's forty-two-room mansion at Yasnaya Polyana, five hours by bus outside of Moscow. He was touring with a group of fifty-one other United States teachers of Russian who had won scholarships entitling them to five weeks of study and excursions throughout the country, and he was enjoying himself immensely.

Teaching Russian at the secondary level was the career Dale had chosen to follow. Actually, he had fallen into that choice almost by accident. Back from a Dutch mission, and recently married to the girl of his dreams, he was almost immediately caught up in the Korean conflict.

He was born with a natural propensity for languages. The ease with which he mastered Dutch on his mission proved that. Following induction examinations, army officials offered him schooling in one of several languages. He decided on Russian, not because he expected the course to be easy but for exactly the opposite reason: He had no desire to finish quickly and be sent overseas, far away from his brand new bride, and Russian seemed to him to be the hardest course, the class that would keep him around for the longest possible time.

He was shipped to the Army Language School at Monterey, California, for a stiff forty-eight weeks of lessons, then assigned to military intelligence.

When out of the service, finally, he challenged Russian university courses and eventually began his teaching career at Ogden High and Weber State College. Very few high schools were offering Russian at that time. In 1964 he was chosen Outstanding Young Educator of Utah.

Dale taught for five years before he tried for—and won—a San Francisco State National Defense Education Act scholarship. The winners had studied for five weeks at Indiana University and now were halfway through their five weeks in Russia. Dale was the only Latter-day Saint involved.

Count Tolstoy was an interesting man. Native intelligence, sensitivity, and imagination were evident early in his life. He was born into nobility in 1828, and as early as 1836 tutors already predicted literary fame for the boy. During his university years he lost faith in religion and prayer, and for the next few bleak years he lived a life of immoral dissipation.

But wearying of worldly companions and the shallowness of a life without purpose, he changed. He married Sofya Andreeva Behrs and thirteen children were born to their union. He determined to live by a code of nonviolence, universal love and forgiveness, and simplicity. Through his prolific writings, his social, moral, and educational ideals spread to all parts of the globe. Few men of modern times have had greater influence on the world's thought than he did.

Tolstoy's epic novel of life during the time of Napoleon, *War and Peace*, was completed in 1869, and it established him as one of the towering literary geniuses of all time.

Now Dale and his fellow teachers were standing inside Tolstoy's home, and his powerful influence permeated the area. The house was a large, two-story, white building constructed of wood. Big by any standards, but fairly simple and uncluttered by American standards.

They had entered down the long driveway, past a huge tree still known as the Tree of Truth where, under its spreading branches, the Count routinely gathered his children together for progressive schooling. There were very few schools of that nature anywhere else in the world. Lush forest growth had been cleared to accommodate the house and surrounding estate. His burial site was located two blocks behind the house, and fresh flowers adorned the grave daily.

As his companions strolled through the mansion's interior, Dale hung back a few steps. Somewhere in the corners of his mind an old memory stirred. Hadn't he read years ago that Leo Tolstoy was introduced to, and impressed by, the Mormon plan of life and salvation? The memory was foggy. He couldn't pin it down, but the thought was persistent. Had Tolstoy really said something to the effect that, if left unchanged for three or four generations, Mormonism was destined to become the greatest power the world had ever known?

Dale is familiar with Russian history, secular and otherwise. He knew that for a period of six months or so in 1906 there had been LDS missionaries in that part of the world. For the Count to have come in contact with them was not outside the realm of possibility, but had it actually happened?

In a long hall, surrounded as he was by the essence of that brilliant man, Dale felt a *need* to know. It wasn't just idle curiosity but a compulsion far deeper than that.

He momentarily closed his eyes. He didn't bow his head or make any obvious show of what he was doing while the others were intent on their local guide's explanations. He offered up a brief but heartfelt supplication that if there *were* truth to what he seemed to remember—if Tolstoy *had* been moved by the power of the restored gospel—he might in some way be made aware of it.

The prayer lasted for only a few seconds. As he opened his eyes, he noticed several doors leading off from the other end of the hallway. Their guide had mentioned a few rooms not shown on the tour. Not that there was anything secret about

the rooms, but there were seven libraries, each one similar to
the others with books from floor to ceiling on all four walls, so
viewing one such room should suffice, considering the
shortness of their time.

Dale walked down the hallway alone. He wandered through
an open door to discover that he was standing in one of the
seven libraries. The shelves were filled with books.

But—the first title his eyes focused upon in that room was
the Book of Mormon, printed in English. (Tolstoy read
fluently in at least six languages.) The book was situated
snugly among hundreds of other volumes directly across the
room from the door, at a level approximately three feet up
from the floor. Next to it rested a history of the Prophet
Joseph Smith.

As far as Dale was concerned, he had received his answer.
The chances of wandering into that particular room and
picking out *that* book from all the rest were infinitesimal. He
was filled with a feeling of wonder; and now, twenty years
later, as president of the Weber Heights Stake of The Church
of Jesus Christ of Latter-day Saints in Ogden, Utah, and
brother-in-law of Karen Gall, one of my treasured friends, his
awe at that moment's discovery has not diminished.

That day's answer added only one more facet to his
conviction that the Lord's church is under His personal, on-
going direction and has been from its inception.

Dale has never lost gratitude for his eye-witness
confirmation that a book that was then considered by most of
the world to be the creation of a humble, uneducated farm boy
is of such quality, style, and content that it caught the
imagination of one of the greatest writers the world has ever
produced.

12

"Niemand Ist Verloren . . ."

Several years ago my husband's company suddenly transferred him to Switzerland for eighteen months and I and our three children were able to go with him. Switzerland! Just the sound of its name sent little shivers of excitement up and down my spine. Switzerland!—the land of movie star vacations and shooshing down the Matterhorn. What glorious experiences we would have before returning to California!

We did, indeed, experience remarkable, never-to-be-forgotten moments, but not on the ski slopes or in some glamorous resort. They came as we mingled with the European Latter-day Saints. We found strength in the power of their testimonies, and courage in their eagerness to help bewildered American brothers and sisters wandering their way through a foreign life-style.

One lovely spring afternoon, my husband and I stood just inside the door of the Swiss Temple at Zollikofen, outside of Bern. The session was finished and we were ready to leave. Somehow we'd managed to misplace Steve, our eighteen-year-old, pre-missionary son. We looked everywhere. A tinge of panic set in, but not really—not yet—because the inspiration of the previous beautiful hours still lingered. Still, with the temple so small, so intimate, where could he be?

A small, gray-haired woman hurried down the main hallway. In halting German, I explained the situation to her. Had she seen our son? As I gave a brief description of his appearance, she shook her head. By now the nagging uneasiness began to surface, and I blurted out, "I'm afraid he may be lost!"

I will never forget the look that softened that sweet woman's face, or the gentle tone of her voice as she replied, *"Ah, Schwester* (Ah, Sister), *niemand ist verloren wenn er im Tempel ist"* (nobody is lost when he is in the temple). No sooner had she said these words than he appeared, as if by some miracle of her summons.

We have been home for some time now, but those comforting words still echo through my thoughts: *No one is lost when he is in the temple.* And I know in my heart that they are true.

13

Arreviderci, Roma

Ah, Italy! Nowhere else in the world are the people more warm, more caring, more full of the joy of living!

We were told that life in Italy is relaxed, easy, unhurried. Never mind that trains leave two to three hours late, or that local guides leave you stranded on street corners—showing up the very moment you decide you've been permanently forgotten. With people so attractive, who bubble so goodnaturedly, how can one possibly object?

We'd adored the other European countries, preferring to travel not as foreigners but to mingle with the natives and take part wholeheartedly in their costums. But perhaps Italy was different. They also say you haven't really been to Italy if you haven't been pinched. We weren't sure we were ready for *that!*

One slightly chilly end-of-April morning, we set out in a group to check for ourselves what Italy has to offer. We were a little edgy. We Mackays had lived in Zurich, Switzerland, for a year by then and were accustomed to a country where trains and business appointments run on split-second timing. Could we operate in an atmosphere quite that relaxed?

There were nine of us altogther. Eight were Americans. Four were Mackays and the other four were friends visiting from the United States—all equally hesitant about tackling a country where we were totally ignorant of the language.

We were delighted when a new Swiss convert offered to go with us—doubly delighted to learn he had LDS friends in Rome who would give up three days of their time to show us around.

So instead of eight fairly timid travelers, we boarded the train a more confident nine.

We were shown through historic ruins at the Forum.

Our necks stiffened as we peered up, up, up at the enormously high-walled remnants of tiled baths at Caracalla.

We meandered through the Colosseum, where brave men and women were devoured by lions two thousand years ago for being true to their faith, and tiptoed reverently through underground catacombs where some of them hid, trying our best to imagine the impossible hazard of life as an early Christian.

We stood within yards of both the Pope and Michaelangelo's Pieta at St. Peter's Cathedral in Vatican City, and marvelled at the painted intricacy of the Sistine Chapel ceiling.

Everywhere we went we felt warmth.

But Sunday we attended church services of our own denomination. If we'd felt love from people in the streets, it was nothing compared to the acceptance offered us there.

Our LDS guides were our friends by then, and they rounded up *other* friends, all strikingly beautiful or handsome with flashing black eyes and curly hair. The new people didn't speak English, but through our interpreters they invited us to dine with them on Monday evening. Dinner would be a combination family home evening, plus farewell for one young man leaving next week to fill a mission in Spain.

They arrived at our *pensione* en masse the next night—later, of course, than we had expected. It was 9:00 P.M., much too late for sleepy eight-year-old Ronnie after a full day of heavy sightseeing. Sensing my disappointment, my husband graciously offered to stay with him while the rest of us went out to eat.

Word of the party had spread quickly throughout the ward, and eighteen exuberant escorts stopped by to pick us up. With seven of us, that added up to a lively group of twenty-five.

The restaurant was all the way across town, but even the trip turned out to be fun. We trooped on and off so many streetcars we lost count, and I silently marvelled at our trust in following blindly where these "strangers" chose to lead.

Our destination was the oldest section of Rome, where red cobblestones swirled in circular patterns beneath our feet. The small café hidden away at the end of a remote cul-de-sac gave the impression of being miles removed from the city. A still, dreamlike quality permeated the air as if we had stumbled onto a set created for Disneyland.

It was spring, and night breezes gently fanned our hair, cooling us just enough but not too much. Strings of tiny colored lights looped across the patio, and the softness of their glow pushed back the velvety blackness of the night.

We ate outside underneath those lights and the canopy of low-hanging stars, on four long tables pushed together in order to accommodate our group. It was after ten—a perfect time to begin the ritual of dinner in that part of the world.

The menu listed ravioli, spaghetti, canneloni, and we eager Americans traded bites all around in an effort to sample everything good this magical night had to give.

One never hurries through a meal and jumps up to leave in Europe. Especially not in Rome, in springtime. We dawdled, letting the beauty of the occasion wash over us and settle gently into our memory banks for withdrawal at some future date.

We spoke lingeringly of our love for the gospel and what it meant to be together, somehow managing to understand each other easily in spite of our lack of a common language.

After dinner someone brought out a harmonica. In subdued, reverent tones he played hymns while we sang, ever so softly, "We Thank Thee, O God, for a Prophet" and "Love at Home" in the quiet hush of the night. We sang in English, German, and Italian, but the words and the spirit blended in such perfect harmony that it almost hurt to breathe.

Nothing short of eternity can last forever, and though it seemed to us we *were* in a celestial atmosphere, it had to end.

We started for home, dropping off a few at a time until we found ourselves in front of the Mackay *pensione*. The other Americans had been deposited across the street, and now seventeen-year-old Gayle and I were being safely seen to our quarters.

We walked without words because our interpreters were gone and we had no way to communicate the closeness all of us felt.

The massive double doors of our *pensione* towered above us by two to three times our height. They made us feel small and insignificant. It was late and the street was deserted. We shook hands all around, then rang the bell to be admitted, and our escorts walked slowly away.

Halfway down the block, one of them turned. He cried out, "Un momento, per favore," and running swiftly back to where we stood, he reached for my hand. It was the youth who would be a missionary in two more days.

"Marizio," he said, pointing to himself. Then he urgently

repeated, "Marizio." It was important to him that we remember his name.

He looked at us quizzically. "Kris," I responded. "My name is Kris. And this is my daughter—Gayle."

A dreamy look came into his expressive black eyes. "K-r-eess," he whispered. "Gay-le." He appeared to be memorizing the sounds as if he, too, wanted to remember everything about this special night.

He bent over and barely touched his lips to my hand in formal farewell. "Arreviderci," he said softly. And they were gone.

Italy had been everything we could have hoped for. But without the bonds of gospel brotherhood that brought us together and rendered language, geography, and age unimportant, we would have wandered through Rome as typical tourists, sampling surface hospitality and glimpsing only a fraction of Italy's generous, loving nature.

One precious evening out of a lifetime; a touching culmination to our trip. Twenty-five lives had touched briefly and experienced a love none of us would ever forget.

14

The Impossible Dream

Some people dream of growing up to become movie stars, or doctors, lawyers, or even an Indian chief. All Ku'ulei wanted was to be a Mormon missionary. From the age of fourteen when she was converted to The Church of Jesus Christ of Latter-day Saints, filling a mission was her one cherished goal.

She didn't delude herself that her father and mother could support her financially. There are ten Silva children, and even in Hawaii it isn't easy feeding all those hungry mouths or keeping that many bodies adequately clothed. Their lack of extra money was compounded by their father's generosity. He's a fisherman. After a catch he insisted neighbors needed fish as badly as he did. Much of the family's sustenance was freely and lovingly handed away.

So the Silvas pull together as a team. Traditionally each working child contributes half of his or her monthly paycheck toward maintenance of the family. Ku'ulei didn't mind helping, but after tithing and her 50 percent contribution to the family, the amount left for her mission account was pretty skimpy. Nevertheless, every cent of it went into the bank.

Time passed, her account increased, and her twenty-first birthday drew so near she could almost touch it.

Then the blow fell. Her mother asked for Ku'ulei's money. She said, "Ku'ulei, we've had a family crisis and we've *got* to have it. All of it, I'm afraid."

Ku'ulei's shocked mind refused to grasp the meaning of her mother's words. No! She couldn't give that money away. She needed it! Giving it up was tantamount to giving up all hope for her mission. She'd worked too hard, and saved and sacrificed too long. Giving it up was impossible! She didn't blame her parents. They were sympathetic, she knew, but they weren't churchgoers, and they couldn't possibly understand what they were asking!

Somehow Ku'ulei managed to get out of the house before committing herself one way or the other. The Silvas live only a few blocks from the Oahu House of the Lord. She had to get to her favorite spot in the serenity of the temple gardens to discuss the matter with Him.

She shed bitter tears during a forty-five minute conversation with her Heavenly Father, and she was convinced her heart would surely break. She expected spiritual reinforcement for her plan to refuse her mother's request, but somewhere along the way it was as if someone gently said, "Ku'ulei, give them the money."

Obedient to that still, small voice, she reluctantly went to the bank and drew out all but $50: That token amount would keep the account active. She *would* begin saving again, but she knew in her heart that it was no use. By the time she duplicated the funds she held in her hand, too many years would have passed. No, by surrendering her savings to her mother she was definitely relinquishing her dream.

She returned to the home of her parents and dutifully handed them the money. Then, with her heart as heavy as a chunk of molten lead, she reported to the Polynesian Cultural Center for work.

George Ellsworth didn't particularly want to make the trip. Purchasing travelers' checks at the bank in Salmon, Idaho, he joked to the cashier, "I'd pay somebody to go for me if I could!"

It wasn't that he didn't enjoy Hawaii. He and his wife had visited there several times before. Now they were considering selling their ranch with its eight hundred head of cattle, and Phyllis was interested in looking for a retirement home in the Islands. Personally George preferred remaining on their ranch, riding his saddle horses to the far-flung corners of the land he loved so well.

But everything and everyone conspired against his staying at home. His grown children insisted he needed the vacation; his wife encouraged; and he, himself, had a strange presentiment that for some unknown reason he *needed* to go. So in the end he relented.

They had a wonderful time, especially at the Polynesian Cultural Center where he and his wife were thoroughly entranced with the color and fire of the native dancers.

In the middle of the evening performance, one of the dancers suddenly stood out to them as if she were sculpted in bas-relief against a backdrop of two-dimensional figures. Outwardly there was nothing to set her apart—she was one of several who wore identical costumes, and they all performed with energy and talent.

Still, something *was* different about that one, and George couldn't identify why. Again came that unusual feeling, almost as if they shared a common destiny. Was there something they were supposed to do for her? George couldn't shake that impression.

The show ended, and the Ellsworths returned to spend the night in their motel.

Ku'ulei Silva drooped dejectedly inside the open, grass-thatched hut at the Polynesian Cultural Center, next to an exhibit of poi in the center's Hawaiian Village.

Normally she'd jump up to offer each curious visitor a sample of Laie's local poi, although she suspected most of them really wouldn't appreciate its flavor. She'd accompany their sampling with a lively explanation of the importance of poi in the background of her culture.

Ku'ulei likes people. She's bubbly and outgoing, and usually she considered every tourist who came through the gates as her personal and honored guest. Whether dancing in the center's spectacular evening musical, or working as a guide and hula instructor in the Hawaiian Village during the daytime, her job was important to her. She wanted tourists to enjoy every moment of their stay on her island. Except that today everything seemed to be different.

The steady stream of visitors was heavier that day than usual, and Ku'ulei knew she was letting them down. The change in her attitude since last night's show performance was like the difference between night and day. Her face felt frozen. Try as she might, she couldn't convince her lips to smile.

She looked toward the curved bridge leading to where she sat, and watched as strangers trooped across it and headed her way. Today they all looked alike. Her eyes fell on the life-sized, carved Kukali'imoku figure guarding her exhibit. She almost smiled for that fleeting moment, wondering whose features looked the most wooden—the statue's or her own.

The sight of the figure's fierce, unfriendly scowl jolted her to a stern self-reprimand: "All right, so maybe you are down.

Don't make it so apparent. These people have traveled a long way. Don't let them go away disappointed."

She stepped to the entrance of the hut and looked around for someplace to start. Most of the guests did look somewhat alike, but one grandfatherly man stood out from all the rest. His cowboy boots and his gray cowboy hat with its flashing red pin caught her attention. She called out with determined cheerfulness, "Hey—you!"

A startled face turned toward her and a voice said, "Who? Me?" His eyes were kind and they twinkled. Before she could stop herself, she had given him a hug. Telling about it later, she hesitates to admit hugging a stranger. "I know I'm friendly, but to throw my arms around a man I'd never set eyes on . . .?"

And the rest is, as they say, history. When George Ellsworth turned to confront the girl who hailed him, he recognized her as the special dancer who had impressed him and his wife so vividly from the stage the night before. As they talked, he asked questions about her life and her purpose in working at the center. She started to explain about her mission, the subject uppermost in her mind, and then suddenly shy, she whispered, "But maybe you won't understand. Maybe you aren't one of us."

George knew what she meant. He certainly was an active Mormon, and he understood her dilemma. George is a special man. He had already helped several young people who couldn't otherwise afford to go on Church missions, and he was tuned in to the look of quiet desperation on faces who ache to serve but can't manage it on their own. If lack of financing was the drawback here, he and his wife stood ready to help Ku'ulei, too.

Over her protestations he assured her he could easily afford the gesture. All that remained was to set up a meeting with her bishop and arrange for the money to be disbursed monthly through official channels.

She knew he was serious when he said, "Now I know why I came to Hawaii."

Ku'ulei Silva is currently *Sister* Silva, one of the most enthusiastic young women in the California Sacramento Mission, or anywhere else for that matter. Her "special dad" flew back to Oahu to speak at her missionary farewell.

She seldom passes up a chance to bear her testimony. She loves to tell in detail how Brigham Young's great-great-grandson was led all the way from Salmon, Idaho, on the mainland, to a tiny, specific spot on the Islands—a man who came at the precise hour of need, with both the means and the personal inclination to enable one of his Father's daughters to fulfill her lifetime dream.

15

A Marvelous Work

Now behold, a marvelous work is about to come forth among the children of men.

Therefore, O ye that embark in the service of God, see that ye serve him with all your heart, might, mind and strength. . . . (D&C 4:1-2.)

Filling a mission for The Church of Jesus Christ of Latter-day Saints in South America was different thirty years ago than it is today.

Called to Argentina in 1948, Elder Fenton Williams, Jr., was struck immediately with the tremendous contrast between life under the dictatorship of Juan Domingo and Evita Peron and anything he had previously known.

After serving in various branches for approximately one year, he was assigned to preside over the Mendoza Branch, in a lovely city near the foothills of the towering Andes Mountains. Mendoza was located hundreds of miles from the nearest Church branch. Elder Williams and three young companions were in charge of LDS religious affairs over six hundred miles from the mission office in Buenos Aires, and they felt very much alone.

Compatibility, resourcefulness, and self-reliance were qualities they soon learned to appreciate. With distances of that magnitude separating them from their president, they were fortunate if they were able to confer with him in person more than twice a year, at mission conferences.

Their first responsibility in a community that knew very little of Mormons or Mormon ways to make their presence known. A Book of Mormon conference, complete with small rented hall and notices in the local papers, would be a start. They set the wheels in motion.

One week before the planned event, they were informed by local authorities that in Peron's Argentina anyone seeking to hold a public meeting must first obtain an official permit from the federal police. Elder Williams went to police headquarters, dutifully filled out the required forms, and returned home confident that they had covered all the necessary bases.

The night of the conference arrived and the missionaries were excited. A number of interested persons showed up and the meeting began. Minutes into the meeting, however, two uniformed policemen and another in plain clothes appeared at the door and demanded to know what was happening there, and why. The Elders didn't understand the problem. They were conducting a conference for which they had duly made legal application.

Yes, the police were aware of their application, but an official permit had never been granted. The meeting was in violation of federal laws. Anyone still on the premises after the next five minutes would be forcibly placed under arrest. Needless to say, it didn't take five minutes to empty the hall.

Now what? The field should be white, all ready to harvest—and they were having difficulty planting the seeds.

Their calling was to spread the gospel of Jesus Christ and to lovingly work for their Savior with all their heart, might, mind, and strength. They wanted, of course, to do it properly, within the framework of this community's laws. The two goals seemed to be totally incompatible. They reminded themselves that they had been sent there by a representative of the Lord, so there had to be a way.

The manager of Radio Aconcagua was always sociable. The missionaries approached him with a request for a fifteen-minute spot on the radio each Sunday morning, for a short religious message plus musical selections by the Mormon Tabernacle organ and choir. The station manager was impressed with the format, the quality of the music, and the deep, rich voice of Sylvio Montero, a good friend and investigator, who volunteered to narrate the brief gospel message. Free time was donated and the program took to the air throughout the entire Mendoza area. It began to have an effect. Elders out tracting were asked if they were the ones who sponsored that radio program with the beautiful music. Everything was going well.

Two-and-half months after the inception of the program, Elder Williams was suddenly called back to the radio station. The manager sincerely regretted he must cancel the program. In his hand he held a formal directive from federal authorities to the effect that no church (other than the one officially recognized by the government) was to be permitted access to the airwaves.

The directive stated further that Latter-day Saints were to be singled out specifically. *No requests by the Mormon Church for permits of any kind will be granted.*

Elder Williams's first reaction on hearing such sweeping restrictions was dismay. Was the work of the Lord in South America really to be brought to its knees before getting off to a proper start? That possibility proved to be quite a blow for a youth not yet twenty, seeking to do his best in a foreign atmosphere many miles from home.

All his life he had been taught to follow the counsel of the prophet, and he knew with firm conviction that the prophet would never ask him—or allow him—to do anything contrary to the law of the land. Far from it. The twelfth Article of Faith proclaims in words of plainness that we believe in obeying, honoring, and sustaining the law. Still, there had to be some way to scatter the seeds.

Shortly thereafter Elder Williams was transferred and assigned as presiding Elder over the tiny new branch of Trevelin in the province of Chubut, far to the south in Argentina's Patagonia. Trevelin was a small town with a predominantly Welsh population which had emigrated to the area because its climate and topography are similar to their beloved native Wales. Sheep ranches spread for miles in every direction.

The branch was small, but they held regular meetings. Close friendships developed between the Elders and these rugged, friendly sheepherders. The Welsh people attended their own services, after which many visited and enjoyed the meetings conducted by LDS missionaries. The Welsh are universally noted for their love of music, and they delighted in singing the hymns.

This new area was primitive, with no local bus system and very few cars. Missionaries purchased horses from local ranchers and joined the majority of the populace by traveling either by horse or on foot. It wasn't uncommon to walk fifteen kilometers each way to Esquel and back for Church meetings or business. Frequently they were invited to visit with new friends on their ranches. They accepted these kind invitations with pleasure, although doing so often involved a fifteen- to twenty-mile trek.

They mingled freely with the natives, staying on the ranches overnight or sometimes for several days. Pitching in, they helped with the work of docking and ear-marking lambs, rounding up sheep, and similar tasks. *Always* there was a barbeque of roast lamb or *asado*. An hour before lunch a previously slaughtered lamb was placed on a skewer over a bed of hot coals. Every man—missionaries included—carried a sharpened knife in a scabbard on his belt. The knife was used to cut off slabs of meat to eat with French bread after it had first been sprinkled with salted water.

The missionaries remember some rare experiences among those fine Welsh people in that remote corner of South America, but they admit they had more than their fill of *asado*. Although they bravely consumed each meal with gusto, few could face eating lamb again for years.

Fenton Williams labored in Trevelin for four happy months and was approaching the end of his thirty-month mission when he received a distressing letter from mission president Harold Brown. The president was bringing a group of musically talented Elders to Trevelin to present a musical concert—a gesture of thanks to the good people there for their kind hospitality.

Elder Williams was thrust into a quandary. Delighted with prospects of the president's visit, and knowing how the residents of Trevelin would respond to music, he nevertheless recalled only too well his painful experience with public meetings and the threat of arrest in Mendoza. He was apprehensive about applying for a permit.

"Public" was the operative word. The proposed quartet and professional-quality concert pianist had presented concerts elsewhere. They'd met with considerable success, drawing good crowds and favorable comment in branches where LDS chapels were large enough to accommodate sizeable groups.

The small building in Trevelin, however, would accommodate only a fraction of the people who undoubtedly would want to attend. There was no question in Elder Williams's mind concerning official response should he go to the police to apply for a permit for a large public hall.

The Welsh owner of the one local movie theater was one of their good and supportive friends. Besides, he loved music. Hearing of the wonderful concert offer, he volunteered use of his building free of charge on the off chance that somehow they could obtain the required permit.

Nervously, Elder Williams walked across the street from his boarding house to headquarters of the federal police and made tentative inquiry of the *Jefe*. As expected, the man produced a copy of the same directive seen in Mendoza and affirmed that he was forbidden to grant permits for Mormon meetings outside of their own buildings.

Elder Williams and his companion, Elder Whitworth, were stumped, stymied at every turn. They were surrounded by individuals they admired. "Loved" was not a word they considered to be overly strong. They'd been entertained in their friends' homes and they wanted to give something back.

Their only recourse was fasting and prayer. This was a no-win situation, but they had faith that nothing is impossible with the Lord. If this concert was indeed his will, a way would be opened. It was as simple as that.

Their answer was not long in coming.

The municipality of Trevelin had collected funds for years with the intent of building a small hospital, and it was a project dear to community hearts. A persistent thought entered the minds of the Elders. How would the mayor of the town, Señor Chaparro, react to presenting the concert as a benefit for their hospital fund drive? The affair would be under city jurisdiction and a small donation could be requested of those attending.

Sr. Chaparro was in perfect harmony with the suggestion. He would handle the details from there.

Large, eye-catching posters appeared on telephone poles and in shop windows all over town and in neighboring Esquel. The posters announced in bold red letters, "LOS MORMONES present a concert in benefit of the Trevelin Hospital Fund, under the auspices of the city of Trevelin," with accompanying date, time, and place. The day before the concert, President Brown and his performers came to town and were warmly received by the mayor. Localites invited them to stay in their homes.

The next evening the movie theater was filled to overflowing. Sr. Chaparro welcomed the crowd and thanked their friends the *Mormones* for their generosity in furnishing the concert's music. Then he graciously turned the entire evening over to Elder Benjamin Mortenson, the group's master of ceremonies.

Everybody had a wonderful time! Approximately six hundred appreciative people attended the concert. They thrilled to the beautiful, professionally performed music and in the process learned more of what Mormons are really like.

Special brands of ingenuity, courage, and dedication were required for young men ranging in age from only nineteen to twenty-one to match wits with the federal government—and to come out on top in a way that brought everybody closer.

The chief of police and his local *agentes* attended the concert, but not in the capacity the Elders had feared. They sat with other city dignitaries—applauding on the front row.

16

God Will Not Be Mocked

God loves each of his children, regardless of race, color, or creed.

Our son, Steven Seither, has always understood that concept, and he believed it while filling a mission in Duesseldorf, Germany, in 1975. He also accepted that there are laws irrevocably decreed in heaven upon which blessings are predicated.

Steve and his companion, Elder Hunter, were invited to dinner at the home of a strong member family. Although the day was beautiful and the meal delicious, a feeling of gloom hung in the air.

Klaus Herzog mentioned a close friend lying gravely ill in the hospital, a woman who faced serious surgery the next day.

She had severe stomach cancer which the doctors had diagnosed as terminal. They planned to operate but offered no hope at all for recovery.

Sister Herzog expressed sorrow at the coming loss of her good friend, and grieved that the patient wasn't LDS. If only she were a member and eligible for a priesthood blessing!

The two young elders surprised the family by responding that being LDS wasn't absolutely necessary. If their friend believed that God had the power to heal her, and sincerely wanted a blessing, they would be glad to do what they could.

That evening they received a phone call. Yes—oh, yes!— the friend wholeheartedly desired that they come. She had no doubt that God could perform works of magnificence. Her friends had explained the basic functions of Mormon priesthood, and she believed it to be the power given men to act in God's name. If her Heavenly Father would only grant her the boon of good health once again, she would gladly serve him all the days of her life.

The two missionaries quietly boarded the tram for what was to be a very long ride to the hospital. Questions and doubts began to enter their minds. It was one thing to tell an active member family that priesthood blessings can be for everyone. But it was another thing entirely to go to a woman dying of cancer and promise her—*what?*

All the way there, they prayed silently to be shown the Lord's will as to how to proceed. "What shall we tell her, Father? She's been given no chance. Have we, in our desire to spread our gospel, raised her hopes too high?" Every passing mile brought greater anxiety and concern.

But these Elders were blessed with a mission president who taught them that the Lord would hear and answer if they prayed to him in faith. Suddenly and clearly the assurance came: *Rebuke the disease and promise her complete recovery.*

Somewhat shocked, they looked at each other and

determined to ask for a confirmation. The situation was much too important—they had to be sure.

Quickly this time, the Spirit confirmed that this particular woman had fasted and prayed much during her illness and was now ready to receive the fullness of the gospel. Her healing was to be the witness she sought concerning the truth of the things she had heard from her friends.

Assured now, the elders nearly raced to the hospital.

In her room Frau Juliana Krueger* eagerly awaited their arrival. She was a woman in her late forties who, despite her illness, was enthusiastic and bubbly. It was evident their coming brought new hope where a few hours before there had been only despair.

The missionaries taught her of the priesthood—how God had sent heavenly messengers to restore his glorious power again to earth, and how men in the Church endowed with this divine authority could bless and heal as in the days of Christ. Convinced of her understanding and sincere desire, they prayed with her and then performed the administration, promising her by the prompting of the Spirit that in the name of Jesus Christ she would recover every whit.

With their hands still on her head they stressed the sacredness of the event. They explained that they knew she had received a witness of the truth, and that where much is given, much is expected. They reminded her that in return for the precious gift of life, she'd volunteered to dedicate her life, time, and talents to furthering the work of the kingdom here on earth. It was a joyful and moving scene. The evening ended with her tearfully recommitting herself and expressing her faith in all she had received.

The next morning staff surgeons began what they fully anticipated to be wasted effort. On the contrary, however, the operation turned out to be memorable. The cancer which had

*Not her real name.

grown throughout her abdomen, affecting all her internal
organs, simply was no longer there. In disbelief the doctors
turned again to examine the X-rays—taken just the day
before—claiming at first that some mistake had been made.
The X-rays must be from an entirely different person. After
extensive explorations, they shook their heads in disbelief and
closed the huge incision. There was no damaged tissue to
remove.

The day following the operation, Steve and his companion
visited her again. They'd witnessed remarkable ministrations
of the Spirit during their mission tenure and they had
expected dramatic results in this case. But they weren't
prepared for the sight that awaited them.

Not only was the patient up out of bed, but she was
hurrying energetically down the hall to greet them!

And what a greeting! To their astonishment she fell to her
knees and grasped their hands, exclaiming loudly for all to
hear, "Es ist ein Wunder; ein Wunder! (a miracle!) Oh, thank
you! Thank you both from the bottom of my heart for this
miracle you've given me!"

They stopped her immediately. Raising her gently to her
feet, they cautioned, "Don't thank us—we didn't do it. It was
done by God, our Father and yours. We are merely his
servants. It *is* a miracle, but one that won't end here. You can
thank him best by remembering your promise to love and
serve him in return."

With grateful tears she responded, "I will! As soon as I am
able, I will thank him properly—in his church!"

Three days later Steve was transferred to a different city.
He was pleased to hear that two weeks after the surgery Frau
Krueger attended a ward meeting in company with the
Herzog family. He felt confident it wouldn't be long until she
was "Schwester Krueger."

Strangely, Frau Krueger never went to church again.
Several weeks went by. The new Elders contacted her

periodically and gently prodded. She was completely recuperated, but for some reason her life-style remained unchanged. Each time they visited her, though, she attempted to reassure them. She planned to begin her promised good works—very soon!

The Elders' visits with Frau Krueger became increasingly strained. Passing judgment on her voluntary covenant with the Lord was not within their jurisdiction, but they were uneasy. Her closeness with her Heavenly Father, which had been her consuming passion when she needed him, slipped further every day toward the bottom rung of her life's priorities.

Thinking she may have been disappointed in the transfer (as is sometimes the case), the Elders contacted our son, and asked his opinion. They dutifully noted and acted on each suggestion, but nothing worked. She seemed to feel that the concern of the missionaries became an intrusion on her privacy. Although her health was now excellent, her apparent gratitude melted away like morning mist on a hot summer's day and disappeared without leaving a trace. Now that she no longer needed help, she allowed herself the luxury of forgetting.

After the next mission conference, Elder Seither was permitted to spend the day in Duesseldorf, and he hurried to her home. Missionaries live close to the Spirit and often the veil is thin. He was worried about her. Deliberately breaking her end of a holy covenant was very serious. He warned her plainly that God works through natural laws and those laws are irrevocably established. Even God himself is powerless to alter the ebb and flow of righteous cause and effect. If he did so, he would cease to be God.

With a trembling voice he told her of his prayers and love for her and of the resultant feelings of dread that came to him. He feared that unless she repented she would lose the protection she had enjoyed.

Her response was a flippant: "Herr Seither, I can't change my life—or my church—the same way I change a dress!"

In the early days of Church history, James Covill, a nonmember, heard the gospel and covenanted to obey anything the Lord might want of him. For this oath he was promised "a blessing so great as you never have known" (D&C 39:10).

In spite of this wonderful blessing, however, he fell away and was lost. Section 40 of the Doctrine and Covenants relates the following:

> Behold, verily I say unto you, that the heart of my servant James Covill was right before me, for he covenanted with me that he would obey my word.
>
> And he received the word with gladness, but straightway Satan tempted him; and the fear of persecution and the cares of the world caused him to reject the word.
>
> Wherefore he broke my covenant, and it remaineth with me to do with him as seemeth me good. Amen.

One year after their last meeting, Steve was saddened to hear of Frau Krueger's sudden death. The unusual condition had unexpectedly returned, and this time there was no reprieve.

17

One Afternoon on Maui

The noise is what Gordon Daniels remembers most—the relentless crash of the surf as waves ten to fifteen feet high thundered against the rocks and filtered the atmosphere with heavy mist, until the air itself was almost liquid. That sound made talking almost impossible.

The sky was cloudy that day—not with fluffy white puffs floating gently in an azure blue, but dark and ominous, and the wind howled its way along the cliffs.

Twenty-four exuberant teenage boys were sightseeing on the north shore of western Maui in Hawaii that afternoon after working hard picking pineapples for more than two

The author's story of this incident was first published in the *New Era*, June 1985.

months. It was their last day off before one final week of work, then a week-long, fun tour of the islands, and home to the mainland. Most of the boys Gordon supervised had travelers' checks tucked away in the pockets of their jeans. They'd heard about a spectacular blowhole set in the middle of a smooth table of rock on the other side of the island, and they'd asked to see it.

They were all surprised. The north area was desolate, not lush or green like the beautiful Hawaii they were familiar with by then. Its terrain reminded them of pictures of the moon. No blade of grass, tree, or other living vegetation in any direction, or even a grain of sand to soften the harshness of the beach. Cruelly jagged lava rocks tapered down to disappear under the edge of the water.

Two groups of twelve excited boys, each with its own supervisor, drove in tandem that day, traveling in a pickup truck and a van.

Doug Carlsen's boys reached the spot two or three minutes ahead of Gordon's. Inching their way down the rugged slopes to the large, flat surface of the table, Gordon and his group noticed that six or seven of their friends were already sitting around the hole with ankles dangling over the edge.

Nobody thought of that as particularly dangerous. Pulling their feet away seconds before the onslaught of water made for an exciting game. Every thirty-five or forty seconds another wave pounded against the rocks below and catapulted a spray through the hole in a pressurized stream of fury that shot up fifty feet into the air, hung suspended for a moment, and dropped back through the three-foot opening with a whoooshh! It was exciting!

The whole area was moist and slippery, and as Gordon's charges hurried to meet their friends they warned each other not to stray to the seaward side of the hole. They shivered at thoughts of slipping over the cliff, but the thought was academic. Nobody expected that to happen.

Then, without warning, a blast much more powerful than the rest exploded with a force that sent them scurrying back a full twenty-five feet into the overhanging rocks. Immediately the cry went up, "Where's Mike?" And one answering voice wailed, "I think I saw him sucked into the hole!"

Funny how different the sounds of the elements appear to our ears after they become the voice of the enemy. The excitement of seconds before now gave way to full-blown terror.

The two horrified leaders leaped to peer down into the depths of the blowhole—and it was pitch black. Driven away almost instantly by the next geyser, they returned again to vainly search the inky blackness where Mike had disappeared.

Frantically they called his name, but there was no answer. Three times the water shot into the air and forced them to retreat, and three times they ran back to shout his name downward against the opposition of the wind.

Between the third and fourth eruptions there *was* an answer, and it was remarkably clear: "Yes, I'm down here, but I think I'm okay." They were weak with relief. With each upcoming spout they'd expected to see bits and pieces of Mike's broken body.

In unison the boys slipped out of their jeans and tied them together in a makeshift rope. Response from below had stopped. They lowered the rope into the darkness, yelling hoarsely for Mike to grab it as it came.

But the waves—the never-ending, frustrating, immutable waves—pounded the shore, and the endless spouting action continued. Twice they lowered the rope and twice it was flung back in their faces. To say that they were frantic is, of course, a drastic understatement of fact.

One of Mike's special friends volunteered to climb down himself, but that idea was quickly vetoed. Centuries of rising and falling currents had smoothed all suggestion of a foothold from the rock's surface. Brave as he was, that idea could never succeed.

Doug Carlsen sat hunched over, staring into the hole, his face a chalky white. "What am I going to do? We've *got* to save him!"

At that moment an object out in the bay caught someone's attention and they could make out that it was Mike. He bobbed up and down like a cork on the waves, obviously unconscious, but strangely his head remained fairly upright and fairly clear of the water.

Doug leaped to his feet, shouting, "I've got to go get him!"Gordon yelled back, "Can you swim?" "Not that well, but he's one of my kids. I've got to try!"

Greg Parker spoke up quickly. "I can swim," he shouted against the beat of the surf. "I'm an Eagle Scout. I've got my lifesaving merit badge and I'm sure I can do it."

So Greg, good-looking, athletic, with lots of natural self-confidence, picked his way across the rocks and slipped down into the waves while Mike, meanwhile, bobbed closer and closer to the sharpened fingers of a dangerous outcropping of lava. With powerful strokes Greg reached Mike's side and pulled him back to the open sea. He grabbed him across the chest in the swimmer's carry. Mike was in shock, and Greg, holding him with one arm, attempted a sidestroke.

But where could they go? If they swam to shore, the pounding waves would batter them against the boulders. Water continually broke over their heads and it was impossible not to take it into their lungs. Brackish sea water is salty and when swallowed causes involuntary retching action, sapping strength from the strongest of swimmers, and Greg's whole system was affected.

By this time they were driven back to twenty feet from the table. The helpless onlookers could barely distinguish Greg's words: "Can't make it. . .we need some help. . ."

A scream tore from Steve Dudley's lips: "Greg's my best

friend!" And before anyone could move, he dived head first into the raging water. Now instead of one boy to worry about, there were three.

But he succeeded in reaching the other two as Mike regained partial consciousness. Later, a typical teenager, Mike joked, "I knew I wasn't in heaven because I looked around and Greg was there!"

He remembered the horror of being sucked through the slippery blowhole by the rush of returning water, and dropping with a thud onto a ledge twelve feet or so below. He managed to wedge himself there temporarily but not for long. The flow of tons of water hurrying back to the sea dislodged his tenuous grip and together they hurtled along a horizontal tunnel and were unceremoniously spewed out at the end.

Now Greg and Steve, working together, eased Mike farther out to sea away from the boulders, and they were comparatively safe for the moment. Gordon turned to the other group leader. "I've got to be by myself to think. I'll be back in a minute."

He stepped behind a huge rock where he could be alone and offered up a mighty appeal to the Lord. He promised everything he had or ever would have, anything God wanted of him he was willing to give, if only He would help bring the boys safely out of the water.

Walking out from behind the barrier, Gordon noticed a small cove about forty feet to his right. It was rocky still, but slightly sheltered from the worst of the waves. Perhaps if the boys could get to that point they could hang on until a Coast Guard helicopter could be summoned. They'd been fighting the waves for twenty minutes and he could see that they were exhausted. Above the wind and waves he heard them pray, "Oh, God, please—help us!"

The boys on shore gathered then, kneeling, into a prayer circle. Gordon stood off to one side. In the back of his head a definite thought sprang full-blown. It was almost, but not quite, a voice, and the words were, "You've got to calm the seas."

His first reaction was shock at the presumption that he could attempt to call forth that kind of power. Moses parted the waters, but *he* was plain Gordon Daniels. The thought of trying something so far out of his realm of identification scared him.

The impression came again and for a third time. "You've got to calm the seas." It became all-consuming and pushed everything else to the background except for the nagging worry, "Will I be held accountable someday for misusing my priesthood authority?"

He raised his arm toward heaven and in the name of Jesus Christ he commanded the waves to be still until the boys in peril were rescued. The prayer circle disbursed and they gathered around Gordon as he repeated his command a second time.

Immediately the surges that had rolled in so relentlessly became calmer. Then two giant waves from opposing directions—directions where no waves had originated before—formed and came together in the shape of a V. Their point of intersection was exactly where the limp and nearly lifeless swimmers struggled to stay afloat. The point lifted and nudged them forty-five feet closer to the cove.

One of the boys had previously run back to the pickup for a styrofoam cushion. He threw it toward the swimmers with every ounce of his strength as a second pair of waves converged in an identical manner and tossed them the remaining distance. Now they were within ten feet of the protection of the cove. Steve caught the cushion and slipped it under Mike like a surfboard, and in seconds they were within their rescuers' reach.

The remaining problem was that the shoreline of the protected area was no different from the rest of that bleak, forbidding stretch. There were still jagged boulders to deal with and the distinct possibility that those miraculous waves that had appeared out of nowhere and boosted them—twice—might also dash them to pieces on the unyielding rocks.

Gordon started to run the instant he saw the V begin to form. He had to reach the cove before the exhausted swimmers did.

He waded in to midthigh and reached out for Mike. As he did, the waves hit again and a surge of water covered them both completely. With hands high over his head, he held his breath and passed Mike up through the water to waiting hands on the boulders above, then repeated the process with Greg. Steve let go of the cushion and was flung into the rocks before Gordon got to him. He was badly scraped on his ribs and sides.

Mike was incoherent and babbling, but all three were out of the water and they were alive.

Everybody felt drained. Roughly forty-five emotional minutes had elapsed since the first startled cry of "Where's Mike?" They sagged against the closest support they could find, expecting to rest there long enough to catch their breath. But Gordon was filled with a terrible urgency to get them completely away, and they started to climb.

One boy remembered the travelers' checks in the pockets of their jeans they'd left tied together on the rocks of the cove. He started back to retrieve them. Gordon screamed out, "No! Leave them. Let's get out of here!"

They carried Mike in their arms, and Gordon was the last to walk out. It was nearly five o'clock. He turned for one last look, and a shaft of sunlight pierced the clouds.

And even as he looked, a new type of wave rushed toward him—not rough at the edges as the others had been, but smooth. He watched in fascination as a black hole opened up on its crest. The blackest part curled over and touched down precisely on top of the jeans (the spot they'd all occupied only seconds before and where at least one boy would have been standing if allowed to go back). When it oozed back to sea the rocks were bare; all traces of the jeans had disappeared, swallowed up as completely as if they'd never existed.

They carried Mike as far up the cliffs as they could manage, and there they stopped to wrap him in semi-dry towels before heading back to camp. Quite a stir was created when they walked in, late for dinner, and in dripping wet underwear!

The local fire department transported the three to a hospital in Kahalui. Their only injuries were cuts on Steve's ribs and some salt water in Mike's lungs. Doctors kept Mike overnight for observation and were amazed he'd lived to tell the tale. Others had fallen into that hole; no one else had ever come out of it alive.

Mayor Cravalhe presented Steve and Greg with the key to Maui County in recognition of their exceptional heroism.

As for Gordon, he still feels a chill thinking back to the hopelessness of that afternoon on the desolate shores of Maui, and a sense of wonder at being permitted to take part in the miracle.

He functions presently as first counselor in the Taylorsville Utah Twentieth Ward bishopric. He hasn't forgotten his promise.

18

A Visit in the Rain

What constitutes a miracle? Often it comes unheralded—without trumpets or fanfare. Ordinary events in the lives of ordinary people take a sudden, unexpected twist. Participants in the drama sometimes act or react in a manner completely foreign to their normal personalities and, as a result, lives are changed—or saved.

Dana Lee, twelve years old, is never pushy. She's a quiet, gentle girl who is eager to please. That's why her attitude that rainy afternoon puzzled her mother. Dana wanted to stop at the huge department store to say hello to her sister Kim.

Sharon and Dana had been shopping, even though the weather was cold and blustery and they would have preferred to be at home, curled up in easy chairs in front of a toasty fire.

Now their necessary purchases were completed, and Sharon wanted nothing more than to head for home as quickly as possible.

It was almost dinner time and they were both cold and tired. Ordinarily Dana would go along with her mother's wishes, but apparently not today. She insisted. Why did she have to see Kim *today?* She couldn't offer a plausible explanation; she just stubbornly stuck to her resolve, which was so surprising in itself that Sharon went against her own inclinations and gave in.

Kim was the oldest of the three Lee girls, the only one married, and was six months pregnant with Sharon and Mike's first grandchild. This was an exciting time. Kim clerked at a major department store, but Sharon and Dana didn't even know which area of the store she would be in on that particular day. She was a temporary "flyer," sent to any section that ran shorthanded on any given afternoon.

Stopping to say hello would entail first going upstairs to the main office to check the flyer board. Sloshing through the downpour wasn't worth the effort. Kim would be through work in a couple of hours and they could telephone her at her apartment. Sharon looked at Dana hopefully. Wouldn't that be okay? No! Dana wanted to see her now!

Sharon shook her head in disbelief at her daughter's insistence, and turned the key in the ignition. Peering through the windshield between swipes of the wiper, she drove the car in the direction of the store's parking lot.

After parking the car and dashing to the store's entrance, they shook the rain from their coats and headed for the escalator. But for some reason, Sharon paused as they passed the elevator and found herself pushing the button. She'd never taken the elevator before. Always she'd automatically stepped onto the moving staircase. Her only rationale, in thinking back to that day, may have been that the elevator is faster, considerably faster than the escalator, and she was in a hurry to head for home. In any case, they took the elevator and then checked the flyer board to pinpoint where they could find Kim.

This time—also without conscious decision—they headed toward the *escalator* to return to the main floor. Why didn't they take the elevator? Sharon has no logical answer. The elevator was still faster, of course (that hadn't changed), and she was still in a hurry to get home. All she can say is that that was not the route they found themselves taking.

They neared the escalator and were pleasantly surprised to see Kim walking toward them. She hadn't spotted them yet. Plagued from time to time with uncomfortable bouts of nausea, today was one of the worst. She'd asked to be excused from her work station long enough to get a snack from the cookie bar on the second floor. She carried a small bag of cookies in one hand and a carton of milk in the other.

Sharon watched her daughter's approach. Like mothers everywhere, it hurt her to see the look of pale weakness on her daughter's pretty face. Fortunately the months were passing swiftly and this stage of the pregnancy should be over and done with very soon. Sharon smiled. Feeling ill was hard, but it would pass. None of them doubted that the baby was worth the effort. Certainly not Kim. Having this new precious life to love and lavish her attention on was all that mattered in the end.

Sharon, Dana, and Kim met at the top of the escalator. If prior arrangements had been made, their meeting could not have been more exact. Kim and Dana, talking excitedly, synchronized their movements and balanced on the top stair, moving forward and starting smoothly down, while Sharon settled onto the step behind them.

Suddenly, without warning of any kind, the escalator ground to an abrupt, lurching stop. Its arrested momentum pitched the two girls forward. Falling head first, Dana frantically grabbed for the railing. Kim's hands were filled,

and in the fraction of a second it would take to open her
fingers and drop her milk and cookies, the chance to help
herself would be gone. Like life passing instantly before a
dying person's eyes, she pictured her body somersaulting from
step to step until she came to rest in a heap at the bottom.
What would that do to her unborn child?

But she had not taken into account the quick reaction of her
mother. Perhaps nobody else would have been able to move as
quickly; certainly nobody else would have had as much to lose.
Somehow Sharon managed to maintin her balance as both
hands shot out to rescue her children—and her grandchild.

With Dana clutching for the rail and Kim bent nearly
double, falling out of control with her head frighteningly near
to crashing against the next step, Sharon seized a handful of
each girl's clothing, dug her heels in, and hung on fiercely. The
force of their foward propulsion was so severe that even her
stopping them was a jolt, but, of course, a jolt highly
preferable to the alternative.

After regaining their footing, they helped each other walk
safely, if shakily, down the stairs. The baby's life had been
spared.

Why did Dana insist on stopping to say hello to her sister
on a day when it was anything but convenient?

Why did they ride the elevator, which allowed them to
reach the top of the escalator the very second Kim stepped on
and began her descent?

Why did all these apparently unrelated actions take place
on the only day the escalator has ever failed in the history of
the store?

I wonder. But along with the Lees and the Haycocks, I'm
pretty sure I know.

19

Six Hundred Stripling Warriors

And now it came to pass that Helaman did march at
the head of his two thousand stripling soldiers, to the
support of the people in the borders of the land...; and
they did think more upon the liberty of their fathers
than they did upon their lives; yea, they had been
taught by their mothers, that if they did not doubt, God
would deliver them. (Alma 53:22, 56:47.)

Could a comparable scenario take place in our modern day
and time? It not only *could*, but it *did*.

It was the night of May 26, 1951, near Sanghong-jong-ni,
Korea. The guard was camped in a narrow valley with
sagebrush higher than a man's head. They bedded down on

hard earth, under tarps attached to their vehicles on one side
and staked to the ground at the other.

Patrols had returned with word of an enormous enemy
force numbering in the thousands pausing for the moment
barely over the next hill. The grim order went out: "Nobody
sleeps tonight!"

Lt. Col. J. Frank Dalley of Summit, Utah, felt enormous
responsibility for the safety of his men. There were six
hundred of them and they hailed from the small southern
Utah towns of Cedar City, Fillmore, Beaver, St. George, and
Richfield. They made up Headquarters and Headquarters
Battery, Batteries A, B, and C, and Service Battery of the 213th
Armored Field Artillery Battalion of the Utah National
Guard. Col. Dalley was their batallion commander.

These "weekend soldiers" were not hardened soldiers
lusting after the thrill of battle, but scholars and farmers,
gentle, honorable men who were also brothers, cousins,
uncles, or nephews—relatives and lifelong friends. They were
young. Except for a few officers, they were "green" to the
rigors and hardships of war. They hadn't joined the guard
because they hungered for or even expected a fight. Most
devoted weekends and two weeks in the summer to training
maneuvers in order to help finance their college educations.

But they had done exceptionally well in training. Levels of
education and intelligence among the six hundred were
extremely high, as was their spirituality. Col. Dalley muses, "I
would never expect to see another group of the same calibre,
with the same dedication to righteous principles, gathered in
one spot again in my lifetime."

Col. Dalley was assisted in command by Major Patrick
Fenton, executive officer. Third in command was Frank's
brother, Major Max Dalley, battalion operations officer. They
were men he could trust, and he knew that they also were close
to the Lord.

This was an LDS battalion. Numbered in their group were bishops, high councilors, and a counselor to a stake president. Like the stripling warriors of Book of Mormon fame, they were "men of truth and soberness for they had been taught to keep the commandments of God and to walk uprightly before him." And they had been taught to honor their country.

Now, almost without warning, they found themselves suddenly called up, federalized, and shipped to the Korean conflict, where they were involved in battles at uncomfortably close quarters and sometimes in hand-to-hand conflict with an enemy so vast in numbers and so ferocious that prospects of returning alive to families in those southern Utah homes seemed dim indeed.

Except for one advantage. Their hope lay in turning their safety over to the Lord directly, and their prayers for his aid were earnest and consistent—all the way to the top. Every morning their colonel's tent flap was lowered for a space of time and they knew he must not be disturbed. He was pleading with the Lord for guidance.

The battalion arrived in Korea on February 16, and in less than a month they'd completed shakedown training and were in the thick of serious battles. Several times they were separated from all friendly forces. In their first encounter, the Republic of Korea units they were supporting fell back with no warning, enabling the communists to encircle them almost completely before the trap was detected. All alone and outnumbered in a foreign land, surrounded by enemy soldiers committed to their destruction, their annihilation seemed a foregone conclusion.

Col. Dalley says, "For moments I suppose I was almost dazed. Then instinctively my thoughts turned to our Maker. I humbly and sincerely asked for help, as I knew and felt others did who were near me.

"The change in my feelings is hard to explain. Our course became clear. All the men calmly and instantly responded to a rapid series of instructions, and in superhuman time the battalion assembled and headed for the temporary safety of friendly lines. For nine grueling hours while we picked our way over rough, steep canyons a prayer remained in our hearts. And we made it."

That was only the beginning. By the night of May 26 they'd already assisted a number of the army's finest infantry divisions, and their reputation as soldiers of merit was rapidly growing.

Yes, they were honorable men, gentle men. They were convinced that they were fighting to make the world safer for their families; and that if they did their job well, their sons might be spared from war in their turn.

The guard established some military procedures that were unusual for artillery units. One such practice was to send out nightly scouting parties, pinpointing the exact locations and strengths of their adversaries.

That's how they became aware of the thousands of troops poised to attack just over the hill. And they were startled to learn that once again they were alone and vulnerable. With no word of warning, their protective infantry had quietly crept ahead in the dead of night, hoping to locate their enemies and surround them.

It was 2:00 A.M., Gordon Farnsworth's turn to stand guard. He was lacing up his combat boots when all hell broke loose.

Four thousand Chinese soldiers, finding themselves surrounded by the infantry, make a desperate bid to break through by the only escape route available—the narrow valley where two hundred and forty men of Headquarters Battery and Battery A were camped. This was a minor obstacle in the enemy's rush for freedom, and the four thousand launched a vigorous attack.

During those early morning hours the fight for survival was ferocious. They fought hand-to-hand in the darkness, but miraculously the two hundred and forty were able to hold their ground against the four thousand, enabling their comrades to continue firing in support of the distant infantry.

At dawn the enemy attacks abated. In the temporary lull the two batteries organized a combat patrol of eighteen men, using a self-propelled 105mm Howitzer as a tank. Captain Ray Cox rode at their head in the open, non-turreted Howitzer with automatic weapons on either side. Following his lead and with guns blazing, the eighteen (most of them on foot) hurtled down the valley. They engaged the enemy wherever they found him hiding, behind every bush, rock, or tree. Numerous machine gun emplacements were destroyed as they fought their way forward.

These scattered, bitter engagements continued for several hours until the opposition finally withdrew, attempting to climb surrounding slopes under an intense artillery barrage by the men of the 213th. That devastating fire convinced them that escape was impossible and they turned back in massive surrender.

With the roar of guns stilled, the artillerymen returned to count the cost. Hundreds of soldiers lay limp and dead, but *not one* was from the Utah National Guard. There *were* guard injuries, but none that proved to be fatal.

Three hundred and fifty of the enemy lost their lives in that night-to-morning encounter and eight hundred and thirty surrendered. Likewise, casualties among the American infantry were tragically high.

But not one man from the guard had been killed.

Before rejoining their infantry, these "warriors" performed a humanitarian act that set them apart as sensitive, caring men. They paused long enough to be sure the enemy dead were properly buried.

A newspaper clipping from the *Stars and Stripes* states, "Certainly few artillery units have ever fought as aggressively at close-in fighting as have these men from the Beehive State.

As artillerymen they are classed among the best in the business."

They were awarded the Presidential Unit Citation for their "unshakable determination and gallantry," and the Citation further stated, "The extraordinary heroism displayed by the members of these units reflects great credit on themselves and upholds the highest traditions of the military service of the United States."

Frank Dalley and his officers—working in close conjunction with the Spirit—brought all six hundred relatives and friends home safely. Thirty years later we still detect more than a trace of hero worship from the men under Frank's command. In answer to my question, "Why were you able to make it home?" they said it was a combination of Col. Dalley's dedication to making that happen, and his common-sense, sometimes unusual military strategy.

But more importantly, they attribute their safe return to the will of God.

So does Col. Dalley. He was a guest on Edward R. Murrow's national radio program, "This I Believe," and was invited to air his conviction that they were guided from on high. He sums up their experience like this:

"Early in 1951 I found myself in Korea in command of a field artillery battalion, with the immediate prospects of taking these men into battle against the communists. Many of them were relatives or personal friends, and practically all of them were from my hometown or nearby communities.

"With this to face, I knew I must have help. I was taught from childhood to seek help from God through prayer. I believed in God as the Supreme Being and believed in the power of prayer, but the events that happened in my battalion's participation in the Korean war did much to strengthen this belief. . . .

"Although the situation was precarious, not once was the outcome doubtful to me."

Col. Dalley *was* dedicated to bringing every one of his men home alive. Striking physical changes in appearance attest to the price he paid for shouldering that awesome responsibility. He began that year in Korea weighing 179 pounds, and his close-cropped hair was dark brown. At the end of the year he went home weighing a slight 147—and the hair on his head had turned white.

For behold, I am God; and I am a God of miracles; and I will show unto the world that I am the same yesterday, today, and forver; and I work not among the children of men save it be according to their faith (2 Nephi 27:23).